PREACHING
1 CORINTHIANS 13

Preaching Classic Texts

Preaching Apocalyptic Texts
Larry Paul Jones and Jerry L. Sumney

Preaching 1 Corinthians 13
Susan K. Hedahl and Richard P. Carlson

Preaching Genesis 12–36
A. Carter Shelley

Preaching Job
John C. Holbert

Preaching Luke-Acts
Ronald J. Allen

Preaching Resurrection
O. Wesley Allen, Jr.

PREACHING
1 CORINTHIANS 13

SUSAN K. HEDAHL  RICHARD P. CARLSON

CHALICE PRESS

ST. LOUIS, MISSOURI

© 2001 Susan Karen Hedahl and Richard P. Carlson

All rights reserved. No part of this book may be reproduced without written permission from Chalice Press, P.O. Box 179, St. Louis, MO 63166-0179.

Biblical quotations, unless otherwise noted, are from the *New Revised Standard Version Bible*, copyright 1989, Division of Christian Education of the National Council of the Churches of Christ in the United States of America. Used by permission. All rights reserved.

Those quotations marked RSV are from the *Revised Standard Version of the Bible*, copyright 1952, [2nd edition, 1971] by the Division of Christian Education of the National Council of the Churches of Christ in the United States of America. Used by permission. All rights reserved.

Biblical quotations marked REB are from *The Revised English Bible* copyright © Oxford University Press and Cambridge University Press 1989. The Revised English Bible with the Apocrypha first published 1989. The Revised English Bible is a revision of The New English Bible; The New English Bible New Testament was first published by the Oxford and Cambridge University Presses in 1961, and the complete Bible in 1970.

Biblical quotations marked THE MESSAGE are taken from *THE MESSAGE*. Copyright © 1993, 1994, 1995. Used by permission of NavPress Publishing Group.

"Without Love I Am Nothing" by Billy Graham ©1951 (copyright renewed 1979), 1997 Billy Graham Evangelistic Association, used by permission, all rights reserved.

Cover art: Escoffery, Michael (contemp.), Circle of Love, 1996, Mixed media, © Copyright ARS, NY. Copyright Michael Escoffery/Art Resource, NY. Private Collection.
Cover design: Mike Foley/Connie H. C. Wang
Interior design: Wynn Younker
Art direction: Michael A. Domínguez

This book is printed on acid-free, recycled paper.

Visit Chalice Press on the World Wide Web at
www.chalicepress.com

10 9 8 7 6 5 4 3 2 1   01 02 03

Library of Congress Cataloging–in–Publication Data

Preaching 1 Corinthians 13 / [edited by] Susan K. Hedahl and Richard P. Carlson.
   p.   cm. – (Preaching classic texts)
Includes bibliographical references.
ISBN 0-8272-2969-0
   1. Bible. N. T. Corinthians, 1st, XIII–Homiletical use.   2. Bible. N. T. Corinthians, 1st, XIII–Sermons. 3. Sermons, American. I. Hedahl, Susan K. (Susan Karen)   II. Carlson, Richard Paul. III. Series
   BS2675.54 .P74 2001
   227'.2– dc21   2001005983

Printed in the United States of America

CONTENTS

Acknowledgments	vii
List of Contributors	ix
Introduction	1
1. An Exegetical Analysis of 1 Corinthians 13	5
2. Preaching 1 Corinthians 13	29
3. Voices from the Historical Pulpit	39
4. Contemporary Sermons on 1 Corinthians 13	71
"Letting Love Loose," *by Charles L. Aaron, Jr.*	72
"Interpreted by Love," *by Ronald J. Allen*	76
"Possibly a Porcupine Problem," *by Dale Andrews*	79
"Love," *by Eric D. Ash, Sr.*	84
"The Excellent Way," *by Deborah Avery*	87
"The Rule of Love," *by Daniel V. Biles, III*	90
"This Thing Called Love," *by Dale S. Bringman*	94
"The Temporal and the Eternal," *by Emil Brunner*	98
"To Have and to Hold," *by Gerald Christianson*	106
"Real Love, Real People…What an Idea!" *by James G. Cobb*	107
"Funeral Sermon for Glennie Iverson, 1919–1999," *by Robert Dahlen*	112
"Epiphany 4, 1998," *by Fritz Foltz*	116

"Love for Mature Adults Only," *by Ken Gibble*	118
"Fidelity and Love," *by William J. Gohl, Jr.*	122
"Without Love, I Am Nothing," *by Billy Graham*	125
"Going Bald Together," *by Daniel T. Hans*	130
"Whose Love?" *by Thomas Henderson*	134
"Wedding Sermon," *by Michelle A. Holley*	139
"Wedding Sermon," *by J. David Knecht*	142
"Toward a Biblical Theology of Love," *by Lamontte M. Luker*	144
"Sunday Before Lent," *by Martin Luther*	147
"Preached at the Installation Service of the Rev. Dr. Gregory S. Cootsona," *by Carol Antablin Miles*	160
"Love Story," *by Beth Ann Miller*	165
"Love: God's Greatest Gift," *by Gary B. Nelson*	170
"Saints Cyril and Methodius, Valentine's Day, and True Love," *by Paul Rorem*	175
"The More Excellent Way," *by Clayton J. Schmit*	178
"1 Corinthians 13:1–13," *by Kathy Singh*	180
"1 Corinthians 13," *by Kirsi Stjerna*	184
"1 Corinthians 13," *by Kay Herzog Tostengard*	187
"The Love Stronger than Death: The Funeral of Sarah Elizabeth Desey," *by Dave von Schlichten*	190
"The Marriage of Debra Torrone and Robert Kilkenny," *by Raewynne J. Whiteley*	193
"Epiphany 4, 1998," *by Joseph Wolf*	196
Notes	201

Acknowledgments

This book is a class act! At its heart, it has emerged from our rich Lutheran history, with its emphasis on the Word of God, the Word of Love, as understood in the revelation of Jesus Christ—read, preached, and experienced among us in community. As worshipers, pastors, and teachers, we have also invoked our responses to the years of sermons we have read, written and heard proclaimed on the 1 Corinthians text. As with all proclamation, our sermonic experiences have ranged from the excellent to the homiletically outrageous. We have learned from these!

We wish to thank all those individuals who agreed to contribute their sermons to this volume and to those from centuries past who have left a rich and sometimes startling legacy of reflections on 1 Corinthians 13. Reading their proclamation is a significant reminder of how minister and congregation seek to hear and share God's love among them in theologically insightful and pastoral ways.

Finally, we would like to thank our colleagues on the faculty of the Lutheran Seminary at Gettysburg, who weekly provide us with much to ponder in their chapel preaching and conversations. Our thanks especially to Dean Norma Schweitzer Wood, who is a constant in our lives as supporter and encourager for such projects as these, and to President Michael Cooper-White, who knows what it means to get the Word out!

Richard P. Carlson,
Associate Professor of Biblical Studies
Susan Karen Hedahl, Associate Professor of Homiletics
Feast Day of the Epiphany, 2001

List of Contributors

Charles L. Aaron, Jr., a Methodist, is a parish pastor in Holliday, Texas.

Ronald J. Allen is Nettie Sweeney and Hugh Th. Miller Professor of Preaching and New Testament at Christian Theological Seminary in Indianapolis, Indiana.

Dale Andrews is Assistant Professor of Homiletics and the Frank H. Caldwell Assistant Professor of Pastoral Theology at Louisville Presbyterian Theological Seminary in Louisville, Kentucky.

Eric D. Ash, Sr., is a parish pastor at Good Shepherd Lutheran Church, Monroeville, Pennsylvania.

Deborah Avery, a Presbyterian, is a student at Gettysburg Lutheran Theological Seminary, Gettysburg, Pennsylvania.

Daniel V. Biles, III, is a parish pastor at St. Paul Lutheran Church in Spring Grove, Pennsylvania.

Dale S. Bringman is a retired pastor now living in San Diego, California.

Emil Brunner is a Reformed theologian of the twentieth century.

Gerald Christianson is Professor of History at Gettysburg Lutheran Theological Seminary in Gettysburg, Pennsylvania.

James G. Cobb is Associate Dean, Admissions and Church Relations at Gettysburg Lutheran Theological Seminary and a former parish pastor.

Robert Dahlen is pastor of Ekelund and Faith Lutheran Churches in Goodridge, Minnesota.

Fritz Foltz is a pastor at St. James Lutheran Church, Gettysburg, Pennsylvania.

Ken Gibble, a Church of the Brethren pastor, leads a church in Chambersburg, Pennsylvania.

William J. Gohl, Jr., is pastor of Peace Lutheran Church, Glenn Burnie, Maryland.

Billy Graham is a lifelong evangelist, head of the Billy Graham Evangelistic Association and longtime preacher on the "Hour of Decision."

Daniel T. Hans is pastor of Gettysburg Presbyterian Church in Gettysburg, Pennsylvania.

Thomas Henderson is Director of Admissions at Lutheran Theological Seminary, Columbia, South Carolina.

Michelle A. Holley is a student at Gettysburg Lutheran Theological Seminary, Gettysburg, Pennsylvania.

J. David Knecht is pastor of Messiah Lutheran Church, Oakland, New Jersey.

Lamontte M. Luker is Professor of Old Testament at Lutheran Theological Southern Seminary at Columbia, South Carolina.

Martin Luther was a sixteenth-century reformer and proclaimer whose primary preaching post was St. Mary's Church in Wittenberg, Germany.

Carol Antablin Miles is Assistant Professor of Homiletics at Austin Presbyterian Theological Seminary in Austin, Texas.

Beth Ann Miller has served seven years as associate pastor of First Presbyterian Church and seven years as pastor of Quaker Meadows Presbyterian Church, both in Morgonton, North Carolina.

Gary B. Nelson is pastor of House of Prayer Lutheran Church in Aliquippa, Pennsylvania.

Paul Rorem is Benjamin Warfield Professor of Ecclesiastical History, Princeton Theological Seminary, Princeton, New Jersey.

Clayton J. Schmit is Arthur DeKruyter/Christ Church Oak Brook Associate Professor of Preaching at Fuller Theological Seminary in Pasadena, California.

Kathy Singh is a second-year Master of Divinity student at Lutheran Theological Seminary in Columbia, South Carolina.

Kirsi Stjerna is Assistant Professor of Reformation Studies and Director of the Luther Institute at Gettysburg Lutheran Theological Seminary, Gettysburg, Pennsylvania.

Kay Herzog Tostengard is a campus pastor at Luther College, Decorah, Iowa.

Dave von Schlichten is pastor of St. James Lutheran Church in Youngstown, Pennsylvania.

Raewynne J. Whiteley is an Anglican priest from Australia who is in the doctoral program in homiletics at Princeton Theological Seminary, Princeton, New Jersey.

Joseph Wolf serves as pastor of St. Paul's Lutheran Parish, Coudersport–Galeton, Pennsylvania.

Introduction

If you say the word *Love* and ask about possible sermon texts, the almost immediate response will probably be: 1 Corinthians 13! So widely known is this biblical text—usually in reference to wedding sermons—that a book about proclamation based on it may seem somewhat of a *non sequitur*. However, though many sermons have been preached on this chapter, there currently exists no individual volume that covers the exegesis, history, and potential sermonic uses of it. This book hopes to fill that gap. It will demonstrate the riches of this text as it may be proclaimed in a variety of settings.

Several voices contributed to this work. First, the two authors, one a biblical scholar and the other a homiletics scholar, have collaborated to share exegesis, theology, and homiletical history for the reader. They are colleagues on the faculty of the Lutheran Theological Seminary at Gettysburg, a member of the Washington Theological Consortium, and are committed to the ongoing process of teaching and writing about the tensive, multifaceted challenges that exist between text and proclamation.

The next set of voices come from the field of historical homiletics: They provide an additional cache of materials for today's preacher. Perhaps the most fascinating result of reading these voices in a survey fashion is that they yield a history of the 1 Corinthians text. First, the sermons show that they reflect and embody the homiletical conventions of their times, such as the allegorizing of medieval preaching, the social concerns of mid-twentieth century America, the mysticism of those focused predominantly on the figure of Christ.

Second, the sermons reveal some of the major issues that have affected proclamation on the text across all eras of homiletical history. These involve the preachers' knowledge of the original languages of scripture, translation of the text–particularly the meanings of the word *love*–and the relationship of the text to the rest of 1 Corinthians as well as to other New Testament texts. Issues of translation and context are also linked to theological concerns of different times and places. A sermon preached on the text from a social gospel perspective is one radically different in tone and intention from one that uses the same text to speak of eschatological concerns. And what do preachers do with a text that makes no mention of God?

One of the most striking features of this earlier set of voices is that the authorship and transmission of sermons on 1 Corinthians 13 have been historically limited to men. Additionally, while preaching on this text today is carried out globally from new ethnic, class, and gender perspectives, publications of such contemporary sermons on this text are almost nonexistent–thus automatically excluding many significant voices. Nevertheless, the selected ideas from a cross section of such sermons offer valuable possibilities to today's sermon writers.

In order to supplement the witness of historical homiletics, a third set of voices concludes this book. This chorus is made up of contemporary women and men who have preached sermons on the 1 Corinthians text from a variety of theological, denominational, and liturgical settings. Their contributions to this book illustrate how the 1 Corinthians 13 chapter may be addressed to today's listeners.

We chose these sermons to represent a variety of perspectives. Together with excerpts from historical sermons, their proclamation of the 1 Corinthians text reveals a multitude of general approaches expressing themselves in such perspectives as theological (doctrinal emphases), moral (virtue and vice preaching), ethical, mystical, practical, pastoral, polemical, and apologetical. Of course, there are no "pure types"; the sermons reflect a blending of these different views.

The *specific* intentions of each preacher, shown in the excerpts and the sermons, demonstrate a unique collage of approaches to text, topic, and context. The reader will find uses of this text not commonly associated with it.

Perhaps the single most important reason for reading the past and current proclamation of 1 Corinthians 13 together is that the reader will experience the company of preachers whose hopes and fears mirror their own. They will read the varying moods and tones of those who proclaimed this text in many times and places and find the awed, the grumpy, the passionate, the humorous, and the pastoral.

Through the collaboration of the exegetical and historical efforts presented in this work, it is the authors' primary hope that something as small as a word, a phrase—as encompassing as a theological perspective—will assist the preacher in fashioning a thoughtful, pastoral, and effective sermon to God's glory and the blessing of the listeners!

CHAPTER 1

An Exegetical Analysis of 1 Corinthians 13

Over the last third of the twentieth century, the biblical reference "1 Corinthians 13" has conjured up images of brides and grooms, walks down the aisle, and wedding-day smiles. Indeed, this text probably makes its appearance at more wedding ceremonies than any other biblical text. This so-called "Ode to Love" sounds perfectly at home in the context of a wedding service, or at least 1 Corintians 13:4–8a with verse 13 tacked on. Those parts of the text, however, that center on spiritual gifts, such as speaking in tongues or prophesying, seem out of place in a wedding ceremony. Likewise, the eschatological emphasis at the text's crescendo does not have much to do with such a liturgical setting. Yet for Paul these core words of love cannot possibly be preserved apart from the focus on spiritual gifts and the eschatological mooring of the text.

Paul never imagined that this text would become a wedding service showpiece, but he did mean for it to be understood in the context of the Christian community's struggle to manifest the Spirit's empowerment for ministry through love. Likewise, the eschatological nature of love presented here has nothing to do with the emotional attachments between wife and husband (after all, it is until death do them part), but has everything to do with the core Christian relationships shared and lived in the body of Christ. This does not mean that 1 Corinthians 13 should never again darken a wedding service. Rather, it means that Paul's words should first be understood in terms of their original literary and historical contexts in order to recapture the reality of love presented here. In that way, perhaps it is possible to rectify the text's vision of agape as that which undergirds all Christian relationships, and not just the marital relationship to which it has sometimes been reduced. To that end, an exegetical analysis of 1 Corinthians 13 will be presented that seeks to consider the chapter within its historical, literary, and theological contexts.

What's Going On in Corinth?

In the ancient world, Corinth was located in a prime spot. The Peloponnesian peninsula (southern Greece) is connected to mainland Europe by a narrow isthmus. At the southwestern base of the isthmus sits Corinth. Thus, in ancient Greece, if a person sought to travel by land between Sparta (which sat in the interior of Peloponnesus) and Athens (located northeast of the isthmus), he or she would have to travel through Corinth. Corinth was also in a strategic spot as far as sea travel was concerned, because that same narrow isthmus separated the major sea lanes between the Aegean and the Adriatic seas.

So if a ship at the time of Paul were hauling cargo between Italy and Ephesus (which sits on the western coast of Asia Minor), it was generally faster, cheaper, and safer to land at the western side of the isthmus (at the port of Lechaeum), have the cargo portaged across the isthmus, and then put to sea on the eastern side of the isthmus (from the port of Cenchreae). If a person's ship were small enough, the vessel itself could be hauled out of the sea, loaded onto a trolley, wheeled over the isthmus, and plunked into the waters on the other side. And of course, who would not want to take advantage of a day of two in the nearby city of Corinth for trade, re-supply, rest, and recreation? So when it came to travel in ancient Greece, whether one was going east-west by sea or north-south by land, Corinth was an inevitable stopping point.

This meant that commerce became the lifeblood of Corinth. Going back as far the eighth century B.C.E. Corinth had established trade colonies as far west as Sicily. By the fifth century B.C.E. it stood alongside Sparta and Athens in importance, and by the third century B.C.E. even exceeded them as the leading city in ancient Greece. All of that, however, came to an abrupt end in 146 B.C.E. when Corinth (leading an alliance of Greek cities called the Achaean League) clashed with Rome for dominance in the area. Rome won, and the victorious Roman army sacked, burned, and razed Corinth, killing its male population and carting the women and children into slavery. For the next one hundred years, Corinth ceased to exist. But before his own violent death in 44 B.C.E. Julius Caesar founded a new city in this strategic site. Named *Colonia Laus Julia Corinthiensis*, after its Roman founder, this new Roman colony was populated neither with indigenous folk nor with Roman military veterans (as was the typical practice). Rather, its new populace came from the lower echelons of Roman society with over half being freed slaves. This made Corinth unique in the first century. It was somewhat akin to an American boomtown in that the city's elite came not from the ancient aristocracy but from the *nouveau riche*. They hailed from families and households whose roots had been ignoble but who had now made it in the commercial swirl of Roman Corinth. By the time Paul entered the city in the middle of the first century C.E., Corinth was the commercial and political center of the province. Its population was more than 30,000 and swelled to more than 100,000 every two years with the holding of the Isthmian Games (a combination sports extravaganza and cultural/arts festival). It had a hyper-competitive atmosphere in which commerce and social competition were the stuff of life as the new elite vied with one another for glory and honor.

Into this competitive social atmosphere Paul brought a radically different message. Paul arrived in or about the year 50 C.E. He came down from northern Greece after having done mission work in such locales as Philippi, Thessalonica, and Athens. Following his typical practice, Paul did manual labor to help support himself and went about the task of founding a Christian community in this thriving, commercial metropolis. The gospel he preached was not steeped in the values of that culture (e.g., power, prestige, status, honor, wisdom, and elitism). Rather, it was the paradoxical proclamation of the cross. From the perspective of the culture, the cross appeared to be foolishness, humiliation, lowliness, and defeat. In truth, the cross is God's wisdom, glory, power, and victory. And through Paul's countercultural gospel message, the Holy Spirit worked faith in the lives of some so that a Christian community was planted in Corinth throughout the course of his year-and-a-half stay in the city.

This Christian assembly would have been unique compared with the other associations and social organizations within Corinth in that its membership cut across most of the social levels of that urban society. Although predominately made up of Gentiles, it also contained some people with Jewish backgrounds. It included slaves and slaveholders, women and men, and folks whose spouses or other household relations were not Christian; though the majority seemed to be from the lower social ranks, some were from the wealthier levels of society. Unfortunately, it seems that people with such diverse socioeconomic status did not check their societal perspectives and values at the church door. Rather, the competitive atmosphere and ethos of the local culture permeated the boundaries, relationships, and spiritualities within the Christian community founded by Paul. This resulted in a fractured community full of friction. Some of the fractures had emerged because of the emphases folk put on wisdom; some because of a spiritual elitism on the part of those having ecstatic spiritual experiences; some resulting from the fact that the community included various "household churches" claiming special allegiances to various Christian leaders; some because of the fact that when the community gathered to celebrate the Lord's supper, the upper echelon were eating (and drinking) with others from their own social rank while the lower echelon (who had to finish work first) arrived well after the celebration had gotten underway. Communal harmony was also being put asunder through a sense of individualism. For example, some of the Corinthian Christians understood the liberation of the gospel to be a license for sexual immorality. Others concluded that they had the right to participate in meals held in the environs of the pagan temples because they possessed mature theological insight.

Thus, social, spiritual, ethical, and theological problems and conflicts were splitting apart the fellowship of the Corinthian community and threatening the core of the gospel message.

An Exegetical Analysis of 1 Corinthians 13

From Paul's perspective, the problem in Corinth was not diversity. Diversity within the fellowship of the body of Christ is a given. It is to be celebrated. Disunity, not diversity, was the problem. Some of the Corinthian Christians had verticalized the nature and status of Christian fellowship. Those who spoke in tongues were superior to those who did not. Those who had more theological knowledge and wisdom put themselves above the less knowledgeable. Some used their theological insights to act in a manner that threatened to lead others into idolatry. Similarly, factionalism and squabbling within the church were destroying the unity of the community. Hence, when Paul heard about the fractious state of the Corinthian church, he took it upon himself as Christ's apostle and that community's founder to write them a lengthy letter addressing their issues, problems, questions, and conflicts.

What's Going On in the Letter?

This was not the first letter Paul had written to the Corinthians (see 1 Cor. 5:9–13), nor would it be the last. This particular letter was written by Paul somewhere between 52 and 54 C.E. from the city of Ephesus (1 Cor. 16:8). Paul had received a letter from the Corinthians in which they sought his views on various issues, including sexual relationships, marriage, the eating of food that had been used in pagan ceremonies, and Christian worship practices (see 1 Cor. 7–14). At the same time Paul received information on the dissension and factionalism disrupting communal harmony in Corinth (1 Cor. 1:11–17). Hence, this letter seeks to respond to the community's concerns as well as the concerns Paul has for them.

The thematic focus of the letter is found in 1:10, the opening line of the letter's body.

> Now I appeal to you, brothers and sisters, by the name of our Lord Jesus Christ, that all of you be in agreement and that there be no divisions among you, but that you be united in the same mind and the same purpose.

Paul is not calling for uniformity, but a return to unity. The divisions (note that the Greek word here is *schismata*) currently found among the Corinthians have torn apart the fabric of

Christian unity. Paul is writing to reunite the people with one another and with the gospel and its core values. In this way, Paul is employing <u>deliberative rhetoric</u> in 1 Corinthians. Deliberative rhetoric is a particular type of rhetoric <u>that focuses the audience's attention on decisions and actions to be taken in the future</u>. Political speeches in Paul's day (and in our day) often use deliberative rhetoric as the speaker gives advice to a council or the electorate on which course of action they should choose. The course of action being advised in a deliberative speech is shown to be in the best interests of the audience and is consistent with its core values. This is what Paul is doing in 1 Corinthians. He is making an apostolic appeal to his Corinthian audience, advising them to desist from the factions that are destroying the unity and fellowship they share as members of Christ's body. In so doing he is refocusing their perspective on the core values of the gospel, in which the cross is God's paradoxical wisdom and strength and the resurrection is God's initial victory in God's cosmic war against death, a war that will end with God's ultimate triumph at Christ's *parousia*.

It is not a coincidence, then, that the cross and the resurrection/*parousia* stand as the bookends of Paul's letter (1:18–2:16 and 15:1–58). Through the cross of Christ, God has thwarted the values of the world and rulers of this age. In the cross and its proclamation, it has been revealed that humans do not acquire God or true status through their own wisdom or power. Rather, in the lowliness, powerlessness, and foolishness of the cross, God has acted to embrace humanity in a saving relationship. Thus, for Paul, Christian unity is cruciform. That is, Christian unity is formed in the cross of Christ and in the form of Christ who was crucified for us. Ultimate unity will be experienced at the *parousia* with the divine triumph over death so that God will be all in all (15:24–28).

In contradistinction to this, the attitudes and actions of the Corinthians have so centered on the self that they are in the process of fracturing this divinely wrought unity. Some are claiming special allegiance to particular human leaders and have forgotten that they are all members of the body of Christ, the one who was crucified for them (1:11–17). Some are clamoring for "special" wisdom from their leaders so that they will be among the spiritually mature and not like the rest of the community. Paul has to remind them that the core wisdom of the gospel is not esoteric knowledge doled out to just a few elite Christians, but it is the wisdom of the cross (1:18–4:21).

Beginning in 5:1, Paul focuses on a number of problems he sees happening in Corinth and responds to the issues the Corinthians have addressed to him. Even in these discussions, Paul usually sets up the contrast between divinely established communal harmony and Corinthian contentiousness, self-aggrandizement, and individualism. Sexual immorality, then, is not simply an individual action in violation of divine law. Rather, it threatens the embodied relationships brought about in the cross (5:1–13; 6:12–21). When Christians file civil lawsuits against Christians in an attempt to gain justice for themselves and victory over their sisters or brothers, they are defeating Christian unity and the righteous status that God bestowed on all of them (6:1–11). A bit later in the letter, Paul uses himself as model (a common pedagogical tactic in the philosophical schools) to show the Corinthians that one is not to focus on one's own rights and status for self-aggrandizement or advantage. Instead one's focus is to be on a steadfast commitment to the gospel and to neighbor (9:1–27; 10:31–11:1).

A member of the community might possess great theological understanding, so that they know that idols have no divine status and thus feel free to attend social affairs held in pagan temples. But Paul understood that such action was sending the wrong message to the theologically uninformed, who mistook the action of going to social affairs in pagan temples for an expression of Christian syncretism. In that way, people were being led into idol worship by the actions of the so-called theologically mature Christians. Because such action threatened the status of one's Christian brother or sister, Paul told the mature that it was important to avoid it (8:1–13).

Paul goes on to argue that participation in the feasts and festivities in those temples threatens one's own baptismal status as well as the core eucharistic unity in which Christians participate (10:1–30). Participation in any form of idol worship means one is drawing into fellowship with those idols and is moving away from fellowship with Christ. When Paul focuses even more particularly on the Lord's supper, beginning in 11:17, the concern does not involve liturgy, issues of frequency, or even a discussion of how we experience fellowship with Christ in the meal (which tend to be our common eucharistic concerns). Rather, the issue involves how the Corinthians have fractured fellowship with one another through the ways that they have celebrated the meal. (Note how the same word from 1:10, *schismata,* is used in 11:18). This meal is to be the *Lord's* supper because he is host, and he is the one who offered himself for the community in his death (11:23–26). The communal celebration of the meal is itself a living proclamation of the saving death of the Lord. In the meal, the community participates (*koinonia,* 10:16–17) in Christ to the extent that the community eats who they are, that is, the Body of Christ eats the body of Christ. Thus, to discern the body when eating and drinking refers to recognizing both the horizontal and vertical dimensions of eucharistic *koinonia* (11:27–34).

Hence, in the letter up to chapter 12 Paul has not only been answering the Corinthians' questions but has also been questioning the Corinthians' answers on a number of topics. Paul sees their self-absorbed, individualized practices and perspectives as a threat to the harmonious bonds that Christians share because they participate in the common reality of the body of Christ. The theological unity of the letter up to this point concerns the needed restoration of the divinely established unity of the community. When Paul turns to the topic of spiritual gifts in 12:1–14:40, the same concern for unity and harmony is paramount.

First Corinthians 12:1–14:40 should be understood as a literary unit. Thus, in order to understand or appreciate what Paul is saying about love in 1 Corinthians 13, one first needs to comprehend the flow of his argument in 1 Corinthians 12. The focus of chapter 12 is not simply spiritual gifts. Rather, it is the diversity of Spirit-wrought gifts within the fundamental unity of the body of Christ. It seems to have been the case that in Corinth there were not only spiritual elitists but also some who felt spiritually inferior. The latter group included those who felt that since they did not speak in tongues nor have special

An Exegetical Analysis of 1 Corinthians 13   13

knowledge, they must not have the Holy Spirit, that the Spirit was bestowing gifts on those other people, but not on them. Paul begins his presentation by highlighting the point that every believer has the Spirit. One could not utter the saving confession of faith "Jesus is Lord" unless the Spirit was at work in one (12:3). Thus, the fundamental work of the Holy Spirit is to create faith in every Christian. The Spirit, then, is about the work of creating unity and faith among all believers. No one is inferior or left out when it comes to the Spirit.

The theme of diversity within unity is next spelled out in the parallel presentations of 12:4–6. Each of these three verses opens with statements of diversity:

Now there are varieties of gifts…(v. 4a)

And there are varieties of services…(v. 5a)

And there are varieties of activities…(v. 6a)

The three verses are then completed with a triadic formula showing the same divine presence behind the variety.

…but the same Spirit (v. 4b).

…but the same Lord (v. 5b).

…but it is the same God who activates all of them in everyone (v. 6b).

Thus, Paul has established his basic understanding of spiritual gifts. There is a significant diversity of spiritual gifts, but it is the same divine reality that works these diverse gifts in every single Christian.

In 12:7–11 Paul makes clear that this does not mean that every Christian is given every spiritual gift or that every Christian does all the diverse ministries at work in the community. Rather, diverse manifestations of the Spirit are given to each Christian. (Note that in v. 7a *each* is in the emphatic position to stress again that each and every Christian is gifted by the Spirit.) These manifestations, though given to each individual, are given not for the sake of the individual. Rather, they are given for the mutual benefit of the community (v. 7b). Diverse gifts of the Spirit are then listed in verses 8–10. These include: a word of wisdom, a word of knowledge, faith-works, healing, workings of power, prophecy, discernment of spirits, speaking in tongues, and interpretation of tongues. A few things should be noted about Paul's list here. First, it is more a broad laundry list than an attempt to cover every single spiritual gift. Second, in verses 8 and 9 he qualifies the giving of these gifts by repeating four times how the Spirit mediates the giving of the gifts. Third, not only are the gifts diverse, but they are also given to diverse people. No one gets all the gifts, but each one gets certain gifts. Verse 11 rounds out Paul's argument here by echoing verse 7: All the gifts are activated by one and the same Spirit, who decides what gifts are given to which people. Thus, what gifts any one individual receives is up to the will of the Spirit.

In 12:12–27 Paul uses the metaphor of the human body to present a vision of our unified Christian reality within the body of Christ. Throughout the discussion, he is highlighting the interrelationship between diverse members living in common unity. By the Spirit's work in baptism, humans of diverse ethnic, religious, and economic standing are all incorporated into the one body of Christ (v. 13). Just as the human body does not consist of just one member but of many members, so too does the body of Christ consist of many members (v. 14). Each member has a different function. While the functions of members vary, this variety does not disqualify one from being a member of the body. In fact, each member's function is fundamental to the God-created health and well-being of the whole body (vv. 15–17). Thus, not only is unity within the body created by God, so is the body's inherent diversity (v. 18). Each is part of the whole; each functions according to God's designs for the whole; each is necessary for the well-being of the whole (vv. 19–21). In fact the members that seem most inferior are the ones most necessary and honored (vv. 22–24).

Thus, Paul's metaphor here is pointedly addressed to the situation at Corinth and is at the core of this letter's basic appeal. Spiritual gifts are functional. They are diverse. They are graciously given by God not to elevate the spiritual status of a few over the rest, but for the benefit of the whole community. Every Christian is Spirit-gifted, and those gifts are to be used in

An Exegetical Analysis of 1 Corinthians 13   15

and for community. Indeed, Paul's claim in 12:25a that God has ordered the body in harmony "that there may be no dissension within the body" returns the audience to the letter's theme in 1:10 by repeating that same word, *schisma*. No division means all are part of the whole so that all care for one another; so that if one suffers, all suffer; so that if one receives glorious recognition, all share in the honor (vv. 25b–27).

Paul applies the body metaphor to diverse offices for ministry in 12:28–30. Four things should be noted about Paul's thoughts here. First, <u>offices for ministry are functional, not ontological</u>. That is, they serve to help the assembly carry out its proper functions. The office serves a functional purpose and has no standing apart from that function. Second, a hierarchy among these offices is also functional (thus Paul's use of "first…second…third…then" in v. 28). Apostles are functionally higher than prophets because it is the job description of the apostles to go and preach the gospel where the gospel has not been heard so that a Christian community can be founded. Prophets are functionally higher than teachers because their job is to proclaim God's word within the worshiping community for the sake of both insiders and outsiders. And so on. Third, it is probably very intentional on Paul's part to list speaking in tongues and interpreting tongues last on the list. This goes back to part of the problems in the Corinthian community. It is not a problem that some in Corinth are speaking in tongues. Rather, the problem is that this has created fissures in the community's unity. Some who speak in tongues have seen themselves as being spiritually superior, and some who do not speak in tongues see themselves as spiritually inferior or inadequate. Paul is not forbidding speaking in tongues but is definitely trying to present its proper place in the life of the community (which he will continue to do throughout chapter 14). Fourth, no one person possesses all the gifts of the Spirit. Indeed, in the Greek of verses 29–30 Paul specifically uses a grammatical construct that anticipates negative answers to his string of rhetorical questions.

All aren't apostles, are they? All aren't prophets, are they? All aren't teachers, are they? All aren't miracle-workers, are they? All don't have grace-gifts of healing do they? All don't speak in tongues, do they? All don't interpret, do they?

Diverse gifts to empower diverse functional offices for ministry are the fundamental design of God in and for the church.

Thus, when Paul moves on in chapter 13 to talk about love, he is doing so in the context of the unity and the proper functioning of the community. There is nothing here about the estate of marriage. The relationships on which he has focused the audience's attention involve life together within the Christian community. In its biblical context, then, 1 Corinthians 13 deals not with the emotional attachment between two sexual partners but with the relational fabric of Christian community. It is being targeted to a situation in which squabbles, individualism, and spiritual elitism have ripped apart that relational fabric.

What's Going On in Paul's Theology?

Before moving to a detailed analysis of 1 Corinthians 13 itself, it is important to note two particular aspects of Paul's overall theology that will have a significant impact for understanding what Paul is and is not saying about love. First, for Paul love is *not* a gift of the Holy Spirit. Paul's distinction between gifts of the Spirit and love is often overlooked by both preachers and scholars, but it is important to understand this aspect of Paul's theology. Spiritual gifts, as Paul spells out in chapter 12, are diverse manifestations of the Spirit given to various Christians. Not all Christians have the same gifts. But all Christians have particularized gifts, gifts tailored for them by the will of the Spirit. Just as the human body is not one gigantic eye, so not everyone in the body of Christ prophesies or teaches or speaks in tongues. The string of seven negatives in 12:29–30 serves to drive home the point that various spiritual gifts are given to a wide variety of people. No one, not even Paul, possesses all the gifts of the Spirit. Love, however, is that which the Spirit is working in each and every Christian. In Galatians 5:22–23 Paul images love as the preeminent fruit of the Spirit that the Spirit is producing in all Christians. Unlike the gifts of the Spirit, which are given diversely to diverse members of the community, the Spirit works the holistic fruit (not fruits) in every single Christian. Thus, while one Christian may be gifted to speak in tongues and another gifted to proclaim the word, both are being empowered by the Spirit to produce the holistic fruit of love, joy, peace, patience, kindness, generosity, faithfulness, gentleness, and self-control. (Note that a similar distinction between gifts and love underlies Paul's presentation in Rom. 12:4–10.) Paul never claims that to one is given love, to another joy, to another peace, as he claims regarding the gifts of the Spirit in 1 Corinthians 12:8–11. Nor would he ever ask rhetorical questions such as, "All don't love, do they? All don't have joy, do they?" as he does in 1 Corinthians 12:29–30. Yes, the same Spirit that endows diverse Christians with diverse gifts also produces the holistic fruit of the Spirit in each and every Christian. Yet Paul understands that there is an important distinction between the gifts of the Spirit and the fruit of the Spirit. When one fails to understand that distinction, one fails to comprehend the full dynamics of Paul's claims in 1 Corinthians 13.

Second, for Paul there is an eschatological dimension to love that is rooted in the cross. Christ's death on behalf of sinners is a manifestation of divine love (Rom. 5:8). To be in Christ is to have been crucified with God's Son, who loved us and gave himself for us (Gal. 2:20). This loving bond that now unites Christians to Christ will never be broken. It will continue into the coming age. Thus, no matter what adversities may come, Christians stand as super-conquerors through the one who loved them, so nothing will ever be able to separate them from the love of God in Christ Jesus (Rom. 8:35–39). Love, then, is part of God's ultimate design. Whereas the law has temporal validity in God's plan, love does not. Thus, it is love that fulfills the law, so while Christians are no longer under the law, through love they do that to which the law points (Rom. 13:8–10; Gal. 5:13–16). Understanding the eschatological dimension of love, then, will be particularly important in comprehending the strong eschatological character of Paul's argument in 1 Corinthians 13:8–13.

What's Going On in This Text?

The opening of 1 Corinthians 13 is actually in 1 Corinthians 12:31 rather than 13:1; 12:31a pulls together that which Paul has said regarding the gifts of the Spirit, while 12:31b presents the transition (and even foundation) to Paul's presentation of love. After the series of rhetorical questions expecting negative answers (12:29–30), Paul instructs the Corinthians to be zealous for the "greater gifts" (12:31a), or more literally, the "higher grace-gifts." The higher grace-gifts are not faith, hope, and love (again, these are part of the holistic fruit of the Spirit, not part of the diverse gifts of the Spirit). The higher grace-gifts refer back to the list of ministry offices in 12:28. As there is a functional hierarchy to those offices for ministry, so too is there a corresponding functional hierarchy regarding the grace-gifts needed for the proper functioning of those offices. Grace-gifts that involve the proclamation of the gospel for the creation of faith through the Spirit's work are "higher" than grace-gifts enabling healing, proper administration, speaking in tongues, or interpreting tongues. Again, "higher" involves the vital functioning of the body for mission. All grace-gifts are important; all are worked by the Spirit; all work for the mutual benefit and building up of the Body and its mission. But some are more central to the Body's proper functioning and mission than others. Hence, in 12:31a Paul instructs the community to be zealous for those higher grace-gifts (especially since it seems to be the case that the Corinthians have been most zealous for the "lower" grace-gifts).

Paul is broadening the focus through his comment in 12:31b when he tells his audience, "I will show you a road that is yet beyond measure" (author's translation). The road (the Greek word, *hodon*, can mean "way, road") that he is now showing them is love. In this context, love is not the highest grace-gift. Rather, love is the road on which all the gifts of the Spirit are to travel. As he will demonstrate in chapter 13, love is the road "beyond measure" for two reasons. First, it is the road for each and every gift of the Spirit. If any gift of the Spirit does not travel on the road of love, that gift is useless (13:1–3). Second, it is the road beyond measure because love will not end at the *parousia,* but will continue into the eschatological age to come (13:8–13). In many ways, then, 1 Corinthians 13 is not so much an "ode to love" as the presentation of the "highway of love."

In terms of structure, 1 Corinthians 13 consists of three interrelated subunits:
- Spiritual gifts in the absence of love (vv. 1–3)
- The reality of love (vv. 4–7)
- The eschatological ramifications of spiritual gifts and love (vv. 8–13)

Love, of course, is the constant in each of these subsections. Indeed, the word love appears ten times in our text (always as a noun, *agape*).

Spiritual Gifts in the Absence of Love (13:1–3)

> If I speak in the tongues of mortals and of angels, but do not have love, I am a noisy gong or a clanging cymbal. And if I have prophetic powers, and understand all mysteries and all knowledge, and if I have all faith, so as to remove mountains, but do not have love, I am nothing. If I give away all my possessions, and if I hand over my body so that I may boast, but do not have love, I gain nothing.

Verses 1, 2, and 3 all bear the same grammatical structure (called a present general condition). In each verse a lengthy condition (called the protasis) is laid out, involving the use of elaborate spiritual gifts without love. This is followed by a succinct statement (called the apodosis) that shows the empty nature of spiritual gifts in the absence of love. In each condition Paul presents himself as the paradigm of a person using various spiritual gifts without love.

The conditional clause in 13:1 involves the speaking in tongues. To speak "in the tongues of angels" is best understood as a reference to *glossolalia,* the Spirit-empowered gift by which a person speaks divine messages in nonhuman languages (cf. 12:10, 28, 30; 14:2–40). This, of course, is the gift possessed by some of the spiritual elitists in the Corinthian community who are using their gift not for the building up of the whole community, but for their own self-aggrandizement. The reference to speaking "in the tongues of mortals" is not so clear.

It could refer either to speaking with rhetorical eloquence (cf. 1 Cor. 1:17; 2:1–5), or to *xenolalia,* the spiritual gift by which a person is empowered to speak in various languages (cf. Acts 2:1–11), or to the spiritual gift that empowers a person to interpret *glossolalia* (cf. 1 Cor. 12:10; 14:5–13, 27–28). In the context of 1 Corinthians, the latter seems more likely, because Paul has never identified rhetorical eloquence as a particular gift of the Spirit (but has negatively contrasted it with the plain proclamation of the cross), nor has Paul made reference to *xenolalia* as a spiritual gift. In both what precedes and what follows 1 Corinthians 13, however, Paul does discuss how interpreting *glossolalia* is a much-needed gift of the Spirit. Nevertheless, without love neither *glossolalia* nor its interpretation is of benefit. In fact, when one speaks in tongues but does not use these gifts in love for the building up of the whole community, such speech is akin to the hollow sound made when one bangs on a copper pot or to the wailing of a cymbal. Because cymbals were instruments used by some cults in their worship, Paul's claim here probably recalls his comments about the audience's former religious standing, akin to his comments in 12:1–3. Thus, he is telling his audience that speaking in tongues without living out of love is not ecstasy, but is tantamount to the empty wailing sounds of pagan worship. Such valued spiritual gifts used without love, which is the core value and unifying reality of the community, become hollow and meaningless.

In the condition of 13:2, Paul adds rhetorical flourish to his argument to drive home his point about the meaninglessness of spiritual gifts when they do not travel on the highway of love. So, for example, the protasis of the sentence contains twenty-six words in the Greek while the apodosis has but two stark words–"I'm nothing." The word *have* appears twice to depict the possession of spiritual gifts (i.e., prophecy and faith) in contrast to one who does not *have* love. The word *all* is used three times to stress the encompassing nature of knowing all mysteries and all knowledge and having all faith.

With regard to the nature of the spiritual gifts depicted in 13:2, prophetic powers refers to being gifted by the Spirit to address God's word to a given context (cf. 1 Cor. 11:4–5; 12:10,

28–29; 14:1b–40). The reference to "all mysteries and all knowledge" recalls what Paul has said about preaching the mystery of God as the word of the cross (2:1, 7; 4:1). For Paul, mystery (*mysterion* in Greek) involves core aspects of Paul's apocalyptic theology (here echoing Dan. 2:19–23, 28). The mystery is God's hidden plan set down before creation, the plan to liberate humanity and the cosmos from bondage to sin and death through the death, resurrection, and parousia of Jesus Christ, the Son of God. Through the preaching of the gospel this plan is now being revealed to humanity. Because divine love is at the core of this mystery (Rom. 5:6–8), knowing the full details of God's plan of salvation without having its divinely rooted love means nothing. The plan apart from love is meaningless because love is at the core of the plan. Similarly, even if one has the spiritual gift to work wonders and great miracles (e.g., to have faith so as to move mountains; cf. Mk. 11:23; Mt. 17:20), but does not exude love in the doing of the miracles, one is nothing. Having and using such powerful spiritual gifts apart from having and using them out of love is meaningless.

In 13:3 Paul presents another elaborate action that is hollow when done without love. Here he is picturing the complete disinvestment of one's belongings, even one's own self, as a way of boasting of one's total devotion to God (cf. 1 Cor. 1:29–31; 9:15). (It should be noted that some ancient manuscripts substituted "to be burned" for "boasting.") Even such apparent selfless devotion benefits nothing if it is not done out of love. There is an irony here in that selfless devotion apart from love would be an oxymoron for Paul. One cannot act in selfless devotion without acting out of love because love involves selfless devotion for the sake of others rather than for the sake of one's own status or benefit. Thus, for the third time in these opening verses Paul is driving home the fact that all spiritual gifts must travel on the highway of love, or else they are useless and meaningless.

The Reality of Love (13:4–7)

Love is patient; love is kind; love is not envious or boastful or arrogant or rude. It does not insist on its own way; it is not irritable or resentful; it does not rejoice in wrongdoing, but rejoices in the truth. It bears all things, believes all things, hopes all things, endures all things.

In this subunit Paul is highlighting the reality of love. This is not to be understood as an exhaustive list regarding love. Rather, Paul's words have a hymnic quality as he presents a collage of what the reality of love does and does not entail. Structurally he opens with two positive statements on love (v. 4a) followed by eight depictions of what love does not entail (vv. 4b–6a). He closes the subunit with another positive statement of love (v. 6b) and a depiction of the all-embracing nature of love (v. 7).

Paul's stylistic touch is also visible in 13:4a as he uses a chiasm (i.e., reverse parallelism) to present two positive statements on the reality of love.

Love
>   is patient;
>   kind is
love.

These two descriptives of love are rooted in the holistic fruit of the Spirit in Galatians 5:22, where they also appear side by side in that list. *Patient (makrothumia)* literally means "far from rage." The reality of love is an immense distance from rage. The concept of *kind (chrestotes)* is not just "nice" but is rooted in scripture, where the word is often linked to God's actions of steadfast love, mercy, and righteousness (cf. Ps. 25:7; 85:10–13; 119:64–65; 145:7–8). Again, the reality of love springs not from our feelings but from God's ongoing actions and attitude toward us.

In 13:4b–6a Paul is presenting the reality of love by negating negative behavior. That is, he presents eight negative behaviors and attaches a *not* to show that love does not behave in these ways. Here it is important to note that many of these negative behaviors are the very actions and attitudes that the Corinthians have been reflecting. The word that the NRSV translates as *envious (zeloi)* is linked back to the word *jealousy (zelos)* in 3:3. "Boastful and arrogant" are exactly the elitist attitudes some of the Corinthians have taken over against others in the community (cf. 4:6,18–19; 5:2; 8:1). In 1 Corinthians 8–10 Paul strives to show the Corinthians that Christians do not live with an attitude in which one insists on one's own way. In 12:26 he informs the Corinthians that rejoicing is a communal activity, because the community is bound together as members of the same unified reality. In the same way, in 13:6 our communal bounds of love mean rejoicing together, not in injustice, but in truth. Thus, in these verses Paul is presenting love as the antithesis to those behaviors exemplified by the Corinthians that are fracturing their unity.

In 13:7 the word *everything (panta)* is repeated four times to emphasize the all-embracing, inclusive reality of love. So not only do all spiritual gifts travel on the highway of love or else are meaningless; love permeates every situation, every relationship, and every activity in which we engage. It is the canopy under which Christians live, and it is the bound of all Christian relationships.

The Eschatological Ramifications of Spiritual Gifts and Love (13:8–13)

Love never ends. But as for prophecies, they will come to an end; as for tongues, they will cease; as for knowledge, it will come to an end. For we know only in part, and we prophesy only in part; but when the complete comes, the partial will come to an end. When I was a child, I spoke like a child, I thought like a child, I reasoned like a child; when I became an adult, I put an end to childish ways. For now we see in a mirror, dimly, but then we will see face to face. Now I know only in part; then I will know fully, even as I have been fully known. And now faith, hope, and love abide, these three; and the greatest of these is love.

Verse 13:8a is often attached to the previous verses as a final comment on love's reality. In point of fact, it actually stands as the opening line for Paul's discussion on the eschatological ramifications of love and spiritual gifts. In saying that love never ends, Paul is making an introductory claim about its eschatological nature. Love will not cease at the *parousia* of Jesus.

That, however, is exactly what will happen to all spiritual gifts. They will cease to exist at the *parousia*. Actually, in 13:8b and 13:10 Paul's Greek is much more forceful than most English translations let on. Here Paul has chosen a theologically significant work to describe the ending of prophecies and knowledge and the ending of that which is partial. The word he uses is *katargeo*, and for Paul it refers to eschatological obliteration, that is, that which will be obliterated at the *parousia* of Jesus Christ (cf. its use in 1 Cor. 6:13; 15:24, 26, where it is better translated as *destroy*). Through the use of this charged word and its appearance in the passive voice, Paul is not just saying that prophecies, knowledge, and all that is partial will stop. Rather, he is claiming that at the *parousia*, God will eschatologically obliterate these (and all) gifts of the Spirit. Love, however, never ends, but continues into the age to come (13:8, 13).

Why will spiritual gifts be eschatologically obliterated? Because they are meant for the between-time, that is, for the time between Christ's resurrection and his *parousia*. They have a penultimate reality. They are meant for the present, in which we do not have full, absolute insight into God's plan and activity. Rather, through the gifts of the Spirit we have partial understanding and insight (13:9–10). It is akin to being a child or looking in a mirror. Children keep speaking, thinking, and reasoning as children (note the threefold use of the imperfect tense in v. 11a). They do not have the mature insight and understanding that comes with adulthood (v. 11b). That is what life in the present is like. When it comes to divine matters we are still only speaking, thinking, and reasoning in our young stages of Christian maturity. Full Christian maturity or adulthood is not something we achieve. Rather, it is the eschatological reality into which we will be brought at Christ's *parousia*, when he has destroyed all cosmic opposition and has handed everything over to God (1 Cor. 15:23–28). In the meantime, spiritual gifts are a foretaste of that future, a way that through the Spirit, God gives us partial insight into our divine cosmic destiny. Again, it is like looking in a mirror (13:12a). In this particular analogy Paul is not talking about the quality of sight, but the nature of sight. It is not that we see dimly when we look in a mirror. (Actually Corinth was famous for the making of fine bronze mirrors.) Rather, when we look in a mirror, we do not see things directly. We only see the reflection of the reality. In the present, through the gifts of the Spirit, we are given insight into God's salvific activity in Jesus Christ, but we still do not see God directly or see God's ultimate plans completely. Such vision will come only at the eschaton, when God is all in all; when we will see God face-to-face (13:12a) as resurrected, transformed, spiritual, glorious, immortal bodies (15:35–57). At that time we will know God and God's designs completely just as God has already known our lives and us completely (13:12b).

Thus, spiritual gifts are a vital and necessary aspect of our lives in the present. In bestowing these gifts on individual Christians through the Holy Spirit, God is working to provide insight into what God is really about so that we can be about the mission of building up the body of Christ and bringing the gospel into the world. But, Paul claims, these gifts are penultimate in scope. They do not provide us with full, absolute comprehension, nor will they last beyond the coming of Christ. From Paul's perspective, we will not need such spiritual gifts, because we will be transformed spiritual bodies participating in God's own glorious reality.

Love, faith, and hope are different. They do not have an eschatological expiration date. They do not just provide us with insight into what God is about; they are the stuff of what God is about in the past, in the present, and in the future. It is important to note that in 13:13 Paul is not telling his audience to abide in or keep faith, hope, and love. Rather, these three are what abide; these three are what remain in the age to come. Faith remains into the eschaton because it denotes our covenantal relationship with God as one of trust, belief, and faithfulness grounded in the divine faithfulness manifested on the cross. Hope remains into the eschaton because hope is not wishful thinking, but is the ardent anticipation and deep trust that God will do that which God promises to do, that is, to rectify the cosmos to God's own self. Love remains and is the greatest of this triad because it is the fabric of communal life both now and for eternity. It is the stuff holding us in intimate relationship with one another as members of the body of Christ. It denotes our actions and attitudes toward all others and is grounded in the divine manifestation of love in the cross. Thus, Paul is presenting an important eschatological map here in 1 Corinthians 13 that is totally interrelated to his words on the eschaton in 1 Corinthians 6 and 15.

Similarly, it is totally related to the theme of this letter as expressed in 1 Corinthians 1:10, because love is the stuff of being in agreement, of being united in the same mind and same purpose. When love is our relational reality, there are no divisions in the body, because the body functions out of and on the road of love. That is why Paul concludes this section with the final imperative: Pursue love (14:1a).

Summation

First Corinthians 13, then, is not a prepackaged ode to love that Paul has simply inserted in between chapters 12 and 14. Rather, it is the grounding piece of Paul's argument on the use (and misuse) of spiritual gifts, and it contributes significantly to the letter's overall theme of unity and the mending of relationships within the Corinthian community. As presented here, love is not a feeling. Its main focus is not the emotional attraction experienced between a woman and a man. Love is the stuff of relationships in our corporate existence within the body of Christ. Love is the reality in which we live and act as Christians. Here the image of a road (*hodos;* 12:31b) provides an important handle for grasping Paul's vision of love. Spiritual gifts are to travel or function on the road of love. When they do, the whole body is built up in love through the various spiritual gifts with which every Christian is endowed. The body functions harmoniously and properly in solidarity. When, however, the spiritual gifts do not travel on the roadway of love, those gifts turn out to be divisive and are essentially useless. Without love as their foundation, spiritual gifts cannot function as intended. They cannot possibly build up the body in healthy ways apart from the roadway of love. It would be comparable to setting an exquisite, finely tuned sports car in the middle of a murky swamp. Without having a road on which to travel, what good is it? How can it possibly function while stuck in a swamp? Similarly, without love, how can various spiritual gifts hope to function properly within and for the benefit of the whole body? What good are the gifts apart from love?

Finally, Paul lets his readers know that there is also a fundamental eschatological difference between love and spiritual gifts. Spiritual gifts are for this age in which we now live, the age between Christ's death and resurrection and his promised *parousia*. In the present, members of Christ's body are in need of spiritual gifts, such as prophecy, understanding God's mysteries, and speaking in tongues, because we can only partially comprehend God's plans and activities in this age. When that final age of salvation dawns, we will not need such gifts because we will be transformed fully into God's eschatological reality. In the future we will comprehend God fully because we will participate fully in God's glory. Thus, spiritual gifts will be eschatologically null and void because they will be unnecessary. Love, however, remains the stuff of relationships in this age as well as in the age to come. It will not be eschatologically nullified, because love's epitome, the cross of Jesus Christ, stands as the groundwork of the divine perspective and activity that results in our salvation. Because love is the stuff of our relational reality in God's future, it grounds and directs our relationships in the present. It is not simply how we feel about another person or only how we act toward another person. The love envisioned here by Paul is the fabric of the relationships we share in the body of Christ, the roadway on which the Spirit's diverse gifts travel for the building up of the whole body and each individual member, and the ends toward which we strive as Christians. For these reasons, love is the greatest of all.

Helpful Studies on 1 Corinthians 13

Fee, Gordon D. *The First Epistle to the Corinthians*. The New International Commentary on the New Testament. Grand Rapids, Mich.: Eerdmans, 1987.

Hays, Richard B. *First Corinthians*. Interpretation. Louisville: Westminster John Knox Press, 1997.

Horsley, Richard A. *1 Corinthians*. Abingdon New Testament Commentaries. Nashville: Abingdon Press, 1998.

Mitchell, Margaret M. *Paul and the Rhetoric of Reconciliation: An Exegetical Investigation of the Language and Composition of 1 Corinthians*. Louisville: Westminster/John Knox Press, 1991.

Murphy-O'Connor, Jerome. *1 Corinthians*. New Testament Message 10. Wilmington, Del.: Michael Glazier Press, 1979.

Schüssler Fiorenza, Elisabeth. "1 Corinthians." In *Harper's Bible Commentary,* edited by James Luther Mays, 1168–89. San Francisco: Harper & Row, 1988.

Talbert, Charles H. *Reading Corinthians: A Literary and Theological Commentary on 1 and 2 Corinthians*. New York: Crossroad, 1987.

Theissen, Gerd. *The Social Setting of Pauline Christianity: Essays on Corinth,* edited and translated by John Schütz. Philadelphia: Fortress Press, 1982.

Wire, Antoinette C. *The Corinthian Women Prophets: A Reconstruction through Paul's Rhetoric*. Minneapolis: Fortress Press, 1990.

CHAPTER 2

Preaching 1 Corinthians 13

This chapter will look at some biblical, liturgical, and rhetorical strategies that the preacher may choose for preaching 1 Corinthians 13–either in its entirety or in part. The crucial concern of this chapter is: *How does the contemporary preacher give this text a new and relevant hearing in the twenty-first century?* In all cases, the preacher is encouraged to build on the insights of the exegetical and theological materials presented in chapter 1 in considering the answer to this question.

Christians and non-Christians alike probably hear more sermons on 1 Corinthians 13 than any other biblical text. These verses have received the name "The Love Chapter" through their repeated use in the marriage service. The only other formal, liturgical position to which 1 Corinthians 13 is assigned is the Fourth Sunday of Year C according to the Revised Common Lectionary. Other uses of the text surface in a variety of occasional services.

The preacher speaking on the 1 Corinthians text must make several significant sermonic decisions: First, in what settings can the preacher use 1 Corinthians 13? Second, what sermonic possibilities inhere for sermon writing in the interactions of text, speaker, audience, and occasion? In other words, what persuasive rhetorical possibilities exist for this text and what specific sermon strategies can be developed from these? Third, which approaches to this text might be profitably avoided? (Possible themes and approaches from historical homiletics in the following chapter will suggest other ideas.)

In addition to the repeated uses of 1 Corinthians mentioned above, preachers also have found ways to creatively use the text in other unusual settings. Oddly enough, this chapter's central theme of love, the heart of the Christian faith, has given it some interesting traveling papers. It has and can be used in a variety of settings that are not Christian in emphases or intent since, when read apart from Paul's entire letter, there is really nothing *specifically* of a Christian theological nature in this chapter!

Wedding Proclamation

The use of 1 Corinthians 13 at weddings, generally ecumenical in nature today, has made of it something of a biblical twin to the often quoted words in wedding services from Omar Khayyám's poem on love.[1] Paul's discussion of love does not name God in any particular way nor does it specify to whom love ought to be directed. This is, of course, a noncontextualized reading of this chapter apart from the rest of Paul's letter. However, preachers may err in their handling of the text precisely in this way, losing valuable, in-depth materials for their sermon. On the other hand, preaching a reading of the text in relationship to the rest of the epistle is often forced when preachers officiate at a wedding where the participants are either agnostic or non-Christian.

What then of the settings of this text at weddings, on Sunday mornings, and in occasional services? It is difficult from the evidences of sermon collections to know just when the use of 1 Corinthians 13 became heavily associated with weddings. A reading of sermon collections from past centuries shows that this might be a phenomenon of the mid-twentieth century on.

But its use probably is warranted for a number of reasons that are specifically Christian in nature. One of these is that this text "echoes" or resonates with other familiar biblical texts on love, both divine and human. It is the perfect coincidence of text, topic, and occasion. It can be an elaboration of the Christian "keynoter text"–John 3:16. It may be used to expand Jesus' judgment on the greatest commandment: "You shall love the Lord your God with all your heart, and with all your soul, and with all your mind" (Mt. 22:37). It could serve as a counterpart to much of the love language in 1 John and is a New Testament complement to the lyrics of Song of Songs in the Hebrew Scriptures.

Another challenge to the use of 1 Corinthians 13 comes in tandem with the use of extrabiblical texts at many weddings, such as poems or readings from other types of literature. The reading of multiple texts can either complement or set at variance the Christian theology that is being attempted by the proclaimer with the 1 Corinthians text.[2]

Lectionary Preaching

For those who use the lectionary, 1 Corinthians 13 is found only in Year C, the Fourth Sunday after the Epiphany. The other assigned texts for the day are Jeremiah 1:4–10 and Luke 4:21–30. In the company of these other two texts, the 1 Corinthians text receives a far different reading than that employed for weddings. Both these texts emphasize the prophet's vocation and burdens.

Here the season and companion texts make of the epistle a form of call and warning, located as it is between the texts featuring the inauguration of both Jeremiah's and Jesus' ministries—"call" because it is a particular kind of love to which the believer is invited, and "warning" in that to love in the manner that Paul describes is to invite possible rejection because of its radicality.

In all three texts for this day, the issue of community looms large. The prophet must stand outside the community, as well as live within it. The distance between prophet and community is in direct proportion to the type of word heard and the manner of its reception by the community. Certainly Paul's words in the epistle are directed at community, as it became unraveled because of dissension. Reading the epistle chapter between the Jeremiah and Luke passages precisely focuses on the susceptibility of communities that struggle on or off the road of love, especially when confronted by prophetic and pastoral figures and their words of admonition.

The use of 1 Corinthians 13 in other settings is almost endless. Because its view of love is not tied to a particular narrative (other than the larger one of 1 Corinthians), the text travels well across many areas. It is only the preacher's imagination and the context that limit the use of this text to typical settings.

Persuasive Strategies: Possibilities and Pitfalls

Creating a sermon on 1 Corinthians 13 is a result of the rhetorical interaction of four variables. In addition to the *liturgical setting* as mentioned above, these variables include: *context, the proclaimer, and the text.* Given the immense play of possibilities here, each of these areas is best approached with a variety of questions.

First, the context. This includes the physical surroundings and the liturgical occasion. *Where* will this text be preached? At a wedding? On a Sunday morning as either an adult and/or children's sermon? In an occasional setting, such as campus ministry or a funeral? *When* will it be preached? In expected or unexpected settings? For example, this text could be preached in conjunction with its use as *lectio divina,* that is, a text that is prayed through by a community. Certainly the setting will significantly affect not only the intention of the sermon but its rationale and tone. Divisions in a church community versus the sermonic marking of a loving life celebrated at a funeral will give far different homiletical insights to listeners.

Second, the proclaimer. The most crucial task of the preacher is establishing the intention of text use. Here homiletical theorist Thomas G. Long offers a valuable tool. Long advocates a twofold approach to intentionality in deciding how to use any text. First, the preacher must decide on a "*focus statement* [which] is a concise description of the central, controlling, and unifying theme of the sermon, what the whole sermon is 'about.'"[3] The next step is to decide on the "*function statement* [which] is a description of what the preacher hopes the sermon will create or cause to happen for the hearers…The function statement names the hoped-for change."[4] Deciding on intentionality is partly a function of setting, but is even more specific. It depends on the listener-participants and what the preacher hopes the text will work in their lives, such as hope, repentance, a deepening of the text-stated realities, a change of heart and life. The preacher can ask herself such questions as:

Will the sermon enlighten? admonish? encourage? create a new reality in the lives of the listeners?

In some cases focus/function statements are already decided, in part because of the setting, such as an engaged couple requesting it for their wedding or its appointment in the lectionary. However, more is at stake than one might first think in terms of the proclaimer's intentions. It is worth highlighting that in choosing a sermonic intention, the issue of poor preaching on this text surfaces. To what negative uses have preachers subjected this text?

Often the text may be used for sentimental reasons. It is here that many preachers violate this text by a noncontextualized use of it, ignoring the major themes Paul addresses in the entire letter. Chapter 1 of this book describes some of the fine distinctions that can be missed, such as the fact that love is not a gift of the Spirit but a fruit, and the prevalence of eschatological meanings. As already noted, perhaps the worst sermonic examples of 1 Corinthians 13, or parts of it, are those that preach love as a matter of human feelings. The love of which Paul speaks is the God-inspired love, *agape* not the *eros* or *filia* expressions of human love. In other words, the preacher is missing the point of this chapter by failing to understand the motivating, divine nature of God's love as the instigator and fountainhead of appropriate human loving. Paul's description of love is far more encompassing and alludes to verbal and nonverbal ways of loving as one undergirded by the reality of God's love.

The preacher may also erroneously understand the 1 Corinthians text in regard to wedding preaching as an effective list of marriage do's and don'ts, a "Ten Commandments of the Married Couple!" In other words, Paul may be made to sound as though he is advocating a list of moral duties. In earlier homiletic history, the preaching of vices and virtues was a fairly easy way to dichotomize and explain a text/situation. Such an approach used with this text, however, misses the complexity of love that Paul is attempting to describe and particularly overlooks the incompleteness of all human love–regardless of efforts–as signified by the last five verses of the chapter.

Additionally, the proclaimer may ignore the balance of the individual and the community reflected in this text, as is sometimes the case in wedding sermons, where the latter is sacrificed or ignored in favor of the former. In a contemporary culture, the need to support a marrying couple through communal efforts is a point that should not be missed. In another context, the balance between individual and community represented in this text is important for groups torn apart by internal conflict.

It is also worth noting here that at some occasional services, particularly at weddings and funerals, there may be multiple proclaimers besides the lead preacher—friends or relatives—who bring commentary to the occasion. Here it is the duty of the primary preacher to discuss text uses prior to the service. This would include what translations of 1 Corinthians are read, what other biblical and extrabiblical texts may be used. (Some of which could theologically counter the preacher's intentions.)

Third, the text. The approach to the text here is concerned with one basic question: Once the preacher establishes intentionality, what specific language strategies will the preacher use to make effective links between the exegesis/history of this text and a finished sermon?

This is a question that involves *structure* and *content*. (The reader should note that this distinction is artificial given how the dynamics of content and structure are intrinsically linked with each other.)

Structure

How will the preacher deal with this chapter? Preach on one verse? several verses? the entire chapter? Will it be a verse-by-verse explication? Focus on a theme? Will this chapter or parts of it be used in dialogue with other texts, either biblical or extrabiblical? One possibility is the use of the "is/is not" framework of many of the verses, which provides another way of developing this sermon; it is reminiscent of plucking off petals of a flower with the accompanying chant, "Loves me. Loves me not." The preacher may wish to structure this text by alternating it with sung or read verses of a hymn on love. Or verses of the chapter could be alternated with other texts. The text could also be used as the structure for a meditative experience of guided imagery. Structurally this gives the preacher a means of developing the intentionality of the sermon through a dialogue of contrasts.

Is it possible that the preacher has more than one opportunity to preach on this text? The proclaimer may institute what Martin Luther called "row sermons." A sermon series could be contoured to the lines of a given section of the church year, such as Epiphany or over some Sundays in the Pentecost season. Such a series might include sermons with such titles as: What Love Is; What Love Does; The Source of Love; The Expressions of Love.

The assignment of the text to Epiphany in Year C of the lectionary sets it beside two other texts, each or all of which form an excellent structural unity on this particular Sunday. The epistle can offer the details of the contents of the prophet's motivation, message, and lifestyle.

Contents

There are numerous ways to approach the matter of substance, of contents. Here the reader should review the exegetical work of chapter 1 in order to create a sermon that responsibly mirrors Paul's own language strategies in the service of good theology. The following list offers some theological language strategies as possibilities:

Word meanings. This may seem too obvious for mention. Yet, as chapter 1 has demonstrated, the meaning of individual words, especially when traversing the dangerous territory of translation, can be put to good use in sermon design. It *does* make a difference that the generic English word for "love" has several meanings in the original Greek, which can make the difference between a good or bad sermon. Explaining these to listeners takes them more deeply into a text that is too easily sentimentalized.

Some of the characteristics of the look of love can also be translated and examined in depth. For example, what is patience? How is it expressed? What relationship does it have to other of the qualities and activities of love mentioned in 1 Corinthians 13?

Biblical dialogue with and echoing of other biblical texts on love. The preacher need only employ a concordance to note the possibilities of linking the 1 Corinthians 13 text with other texts. In fact, the preacher may choose to read an "echo text" alongside the Corinthians verses as a means of letting the two texts work on each other in the listener's mind.

This is also a time to think of using biblical texts that are not ordinarily considered in company with the Corinthians work. Certainly, many listeners are long overdue in hearing a healthy, incarnational link between this text and verses from the Song of Songs.

If either lectionary-based texts or other texts are chosen, the preacher is given wide latitude theologically to develop the Corinthians text in unique ways, such as focusing on themes of justice, evangelism, and stewardship. The text may be used as a blueprint for the reality of how daily Christian vocation is lived out.

Thematic development. Several major theological topics emerge from 1 Corinthians 13 as preaching possibilities (and this is only a starting list): the varied meanings of love; the nature and mysteries of God's love (as compared with that of human love); love as obedience, a radical way of life; the meanings of sacrifice; the eschatological view of human love and community; human finitude; the function and role of the gifts and the fruit of the Spirit in faith communities; dissension and reconciliation; the role of faith and knowledge in relationship to love.

The preacher may also choose to focus on major *theological topics:* the nature of God, the mighty acts of God; christologically, to describe the meanings of the life, death, and resurrection of Jesus Christ and also the ongoing work of the Spirit in multifaceted ways in the world.

Or the preacher may speak *anthropologically,* creating proclamation that is highly appropriate not only for settings pertaining to the individual but for communities, as Paul intended—particularly communities that are in trouble. It is here that the original intention of Paul's letter may become highly useful to the preacher facing groups in conflicted settings.

Metaphors. Paul uses two major metaphors of growth and vision, and even these are interrelated. The preacher can develop these theologically and topically. Growth in love is described, in part, through terms of adult and childish actions and is related to the development of vision. Another way of approaching the same thing is to speak of maturation in love in terms of immaturity or insufficient knowledge. Adult/child and partial/full sight–knowledge are two similes used to describe the always-incomplete ability of humanity to love fully and well. Paul arrives at his definition of love by using the *via negativa.*

The first chapter also describes another implicit metaphor in this work, the enactment of love/loving as a road–possibly a journey. Paul's audience, the household of faith (specified as the church in Corinth) can be turned into a metaphor. What rules, laws, dynamics, and responses govern this peculiar household? How do we create the household of faith today in the manner of God's agape?

If the preacher wishes to use drama as an enactment of this passage, particularly with child participants, love could be personified in different ways. What would a "Patience" look and sound like, for example? Such personification certainly follows from a long and respectable homiletical history, such as the work of John Bunyan and C. S. Lewis.

Exploring other theological features: Some of these have been discussed in differing ways in chapter 1. Enlarging on the balance between the "I" and the "We," the preacher can note that Paul uses the personal pronoun *I* (vv. 1–3, 11, 12b: The use of *I* is in terms of negation or incompleteness: "If I speak....If I have prophetic powers...if I have faith...if I give away possessions...if I give away all my possessions." What are the checks and balances that place the I and the community in relationship to each other? What happens when the "Me, Myself, and I" meet community?

Chapter 13's very structure and themes represent human loving as fragmentary and cast on an eternal trajectory. With Paul's statement at the beginning of verse 8, "Love never ends," the remaining verses, through comparison and contrast, describe love in eschatological terms; *all* gifts and responses are regarded, finally, as only partial. Even adult maturity and a sense of clarity of vision emphasize the fact that experiencing self and others through love is at best only fragile, incomplete. Only God knows the loving self or the self that attempts to love. Love, at its best or worst, is finally inchoate in human terms and awaits the "clearing of the decks" of all hindrances for the continuance of its true and fullest expression in the end times.

An emphasis on eschatology in relationship to this chapter could contrast the daily efforts of loving with their eternal meaning. In a sermon collection by John Henry Newman[5] he often repeats the theme of those neglecting the daily call to holiness, with the result being that the individual's failure to develop the habit of loving over a lifetime would result in being *uncomfortable* in God's heaven! In chapter 4, an excerpt from John Calvin also comments wryly on what it means for the ultimate dismissal of faith and knowledge from the eternal stage, leaving only love.

Conclusion

This chapter has described the need to attend to the setting in which the preacher wishes to share the 1 Corinthians 13 text. The preacher must be alert to the context in which the rhetorical dynamics of setting, text, and proclaimer interact with one another.

A primary task of the preacher in creating a fittingly contextualized sermon is addressing intentionality. This is basic to creating a sermon that has biblical, theological, and homiletical integrity. Establishing a clear intention for the sermon involves looking at what long has been described as the *focus* of the text for the sermon and its hoped-for *functioning* or activity among the listeners. The persuasive strategies of the preacher will only work effectively if intentionality is clearly understood by both preacher and listeners. This is particularly important for a text that listeners are often accustomed to framing in only one major way, such as hearing chapter 13 as part of a wedding sermon. Clarity of intention will enable such listeners to receive the chapter in new ways.

CHAPTER 3

Voices from the Historical Pulpit

A Chameleon Text

A survey of the homiletical history of 1 Corinthians 13 yields some surprising results. Whether examining the sermon collections of the patristic era or the current century, proclamation on this text is rarely included. Why is this? There are some factual reasons and also some speculative possibilities.

Some specific realities governed the appearance of the 1 Corinthians text. First, in the early church, sermon methodology was not governed by an organized lectionary. The preaching "fathers" were free to select from a rich, though yet-evolving history that offered proclamation through the lenses of the primary christological festivals and themes, apologetics, and the commemoration of the saints. Their sermons were rarely preached on a single text, but focused more through a cross-referencing of multiple biblical texts within a given sermon. Second, the most obvious problem connected with finding sermons on 1 Corinthians 13 simply has to do with archival and translation realities: The majority of preached sermons from the earliest decades of the church are lost to us. Third, the majority of sermons in almost any era privileges the preaching of materials from the gospel over the epistles.

Other possible reasons for the dearth of sermons on this chapter–albeit speculative–can be deduced from the social and religious contexts of the varied eras of proclamation. Given the sensitivity to rhetoric displayed in the earlier eras of homiletical history, it is possible that the chapter may have been under suspicion for its persuasive speech on love, which lacked any reference to God or to the Christian faith.

Theologically speaking, this Pauline chapter is a liturgical and ecclesiastical vector that is subject to hermeneutical issues aligning it either with highly sacramental or charismatic traditions of preaching over the centuries. The original setting of the thirteenth chapter appears squarely in the middle of a Pauline discussion on evolving church traditions, a discussion that uses the term *agape* to describe the love feasts of the community. This connection with sacramental theology may have posed difficulties that preachers deemed irrelevant to their circumstances and could be a factor in its infrequent proclamatory appearances in some traditions.

Another possible reason for its minimal published appearances may have to do with translations. How exactly were this chapter and the word *love* heard over the centuries? How have preachers interpreted the original Greek sense of *agape* when the phrase was translated into other languages? The confluence of topics and translation also raises the question of how the word *charity* or *love* preached in different eras in terms of the connections (if made) between love feasts and almsgiving. In earlier English translations, primarily the King James translation, did the use of the word *charity* shift textual meanings to more of an anthropological venture than a God-derived one? Sermon texts using the word *charity* also reveal that it is defined both as an affective reality and as an activity.

In a footnote in an edition of John Calvin's commentary on 1 Corinthians and the thirteenth chapter, nineteenth-century translator Reverend John Pringle footnoted this comment.

> *Penn,* in his *Annotations,* gives the following account of the term *charity,* as made use of in our English translation–"If the Latin version had not rendered *"agape"* in this place, by *"charitas,"* instead of *"amor-love,"* we should not have found the word *"charity"* in our English version. But Wiclif, who only knew the Latin Scripture, adopted from it that word, and rendered, "and I have not *charite."* When the knowledge of the Greek was acquired by our learned Reformers, the first revisers of Wiclif were sensible of the

unsuitableness of this translation, and rendered this clause–"and yet had no *love,*" as it is printed in the *"Newe Testament in Englishe and Latin, of 1548";* and they rendered *"agape-love"* throughout this chapter. Our last revisers abandoned this sound correction of their immediate predecessors, and brought back the Latinising "charity" of Wicliff, who was only excusable for employing that word, because he translated from a Latin text, in ignorance of its Greek original."[1]

Two other possible factors may account for few available sermons on 1 Corinthians 13. An examination of more substantial records and collections of sermons from the nineteenth century shows that popular preaching topics generally addressed the gospel's key message with emphases on eschatology and salvation; the weight of the available sermon collections shows that these took priority over matters of ecclesiology and church community. Sermons on texts from 2 Corinthians, for example, are much in evidence and use verses that highlight death and resurrection and the deity of Christ. This is not surprising in a psychological and social sense, given the generally high mortality rates and lower life expectancy levels of the time.

It is also feasible to suggest that the issues Paul is addressing in relationship to charismatic *gifts* of the Spirit may be viewed as less important in many instances of preaching over the centuries. This is so for two reasons. First, the emphasis on the *fruit* of the Spirit relates more obviously to the predominance of preaching the "virtues" of the Christian life. This was a comfortable alliance for many preachers educated in Greek and Roman philosophy that stressed the same or similar matters. Second, was it even contextually meaningful to address such concerns as Paul is raising in chapter 13 with any frequency outside the context of more recent developments historically with Pentecostal movements?

From Snippets to Sermons

The field of historical homiletics yields a variety of sermonic material on 1 Corinthians 13 from preachers of many times, places, and theological perspectives. The rationale for including the following material is to provide the contemporary proclaimer with potential ideas and approaches. Materials have been divided between this chapter and the next with proclamatory materials in this chapter taken from the earliest church records through the end of the eighteenth century. The remainder of sermon materials in chapter 4 covers the archival bulk of what is available from the nineteenth through the twenty-first centuries.

Certainly, theological and stylistic differences emerging from various homiletical eras are, at some points, nontransferable. For example, the reader will note occasional references to then-contemporary events for illustrative materials, archaic word usage, or theological debates of the time. While the sermonic styles in which some of the works are presented may be outdated from a contemporary perspective, if they are read in their own historical context, they may yet provide the reader with the needed word or image for a contemporary sermon. The quoted sermon materials that follow are filled with elegant, lively theological proclamation that has endured across the centuries because of the discerning eye of the pastoral theologians for the true nature of the human condition.

Proclamatory responses to 1 Corinthians 13 are sermonic in a variety of forms besides the fully developed sermon form. There are brief paragraphs composed by the patristic preachers both in their commentaries and general proclamation (the line is narrow between these two in many cases) and borrowed by other preachers. The role of the "postil" or biblical commentary sometimes results in offerings of "Aids for the Preacher," as is the case at the end of Karl Barth's *Church Dogmatics*. Chapter 13 is also frequently preached as part of a topical approach to love and/or charity and is expressed by preachers in both lectionary and occasional format. Terminology used to describe preaching may be, variously, *address, sermon, homily, tractate, meditation,* and even *lecture.*

Sermonic materials are arranged in rough chronological order and scrutinized according to these factors (when available):

- The author, title, and identified preaching section of the text
- The liturgical setting and/or audience for the sermon
- The sermon's main intention/issue/problem
- The major structural aspects of the sermon
- Language strategies used by the preacher, including quotes that highlight passages crucial to the argument of the sermon or significant in their aesthetic appeal and suggestiveness for contemporary proclaimers

The idea for a contemporary sermon may possibly be found in elements listed in any of these five categories. In some cases the preachers provide some very surprising possibilities!

The Preachers Speak

Augustine (354–430 C.E.)

This sermon is entitled in a recent translation "On the Reading of the Apostle, 1 Corinthians 12:31–13:31, where he says: *I will show you a superlative way;* against the Donatists." It was preached in June, 404, in Carthage.[2]

The sermon is based on the use of the text in an uncommon way for contemporary times. It is employed as a polemic against the Donatists. The text is also a type of apology and a means of further evangelizing the listeners, since Augustine takes pains to educate his listeners about basic definitions and aspects of the faith.

Augustine's intention is to highlight elements related to charity and prophecy. Actual attention to the text is scanty and appears only at the beginning. Structurally, Augustine uses the text as a springboard for raising a variety of related texts and issues in his efforts to combat heresy: faith, the metaphor of the body of Christ, the place of the Donatists in the church at the time, accusations against Crispinus, an invitation to the Donatists to return to the Catholic church, and references to the Pentecost event.

Augustine's use of the text suggests that it could be preached today as a means of evangelism for faith seekers and even a counter to other contemporary theological heresies and fads. It is a warning to preachers to consider the fact that heresy is a constant threat to the faithful and not merely an event of historical record.

His language strategies employ a variety of Old and New Testament supporting texts, personal pleas to the heretics, admonition, theological definitions, and two major metaphors: the grafting of the wild olive branches and the body of Christ. One language strategy is to play off people's theological assumptions through use of paired concepts. "What about faith? Can we find anybody who also has faith, and hasn't got charity? There are many people who believe and don't love. There's no point in counting all the human beings; we find that the demons have believed what we believe and don't love what we love…So we find it is possible for someone also to have faith, and not have charity."[3]

John Chrysostom (347–407 C.E.)

Two of John Chrysostom's homilies on 1 Corinthians 13 offer some rich phrases for homiletical consideration today. No information is available on either the date or audience for the homilies.

The first homily, "Homily XXXIII,"[4] designates verse 4 as its focus, but actually ranges over a number of verses. A key homiletical technique is the use of an accumulation of both Old and New Testament examples to illustrate the verses discussed.

Chrysostom understands clearly the psychological motivations of humanity in his comment on love as being kind: "For since there are some who practice their long-suffering with a view not to their own self-denial, but to the punishment of those who have provoked them, to make them burst with wrath; he [Paul] saith that neither hath charity this defect."[5]

The second homily is entitled "Homily XXXIV, 1 Corinthian 13, 8."[6] Chrysostom's intention at the beginning of the sermon is to lead the listener through the text, and he does so, covering most of the verses in the chapter. The materials are not developed in depth but do contain interesting phrases and concepts.

In relation to seeing through a glass or mirror, Chrysostom comments on the *content*, what we might see of God: "Not as though God hath a face...but to express the notion of greater clearness and perspicuity."[7] He understands Paul to be meaning: "*Follow after love.* For there is surely need of *following*, and a kind of vehement running after her: in such sort doth she fly from us, and so many are the things which trip us up in that direction. Wherefore we have ever need of great earnestness in order to overtake her. And to point out this, Paul said not, *follow love,* but *pursue* her; stirring us up, and inflaming us to lay hold on her."[8]

The preacher's personification of love as a desirable yet elusive presence in the life of the believer demonstrates the strenuous measures needed for living a life of active love.

Saint Caesarius, Bishop of Arles (470–543 C.E.)

Saint Caesarius reflects the typical patristic era of sermonic borrowing; many of his ideas, quotes, and sermon materials are borrowed from Augustine. He quotes 1 Corinthians 13 infrequently and then usually in the context of the topic "charity." The verse he repeats most often from the chapter is 13:3. Two of Caesarius' sermons are worth noting on the matter of charity.

In Sermon 23[9] Caesarius weighs charity against its other extreme: "Nothing is so adverse to and contrary to charity, which is the foundation of all virtues, as avarice, which is the root of all evils."[10] He is pastoral in noting that keeping the law is not necessarily being charitable and also that failing to fulfill the law is also not necessarily a failure of charity but rather a weakness of the human being.

Caesarius personifies true charity at the sermon's conclusion by noting that:

> It is strong in difficult sufferings, cheerful in good works, very secure in temptation, most pleasant among true brothers, exceedingly patient among the false...Its company does not entail bitterness, its conversation bears no deceit. If you are willing to observe it wholeheartedly, it will make you joyfully fulfill God's

commands in this life and obtain eternal rewards in the world to come.[11]

Sermon 29 was obviously written in an absence from his congregation. Caesarius notes that despite this fact, "Indeed, two people who love each other with a holy affection are so united by a binding charity that they can never be separated."[12] The sermon variously treats charity as something to possess, something to practice, and something that invites refuge and will actively create changes in the life of the seeker.

This sermon contains an analogy comparing charity with oil.

> Just as oil is known to be better than all liquids, so charity is more noble than all the virtues. If a man has infinite riches but no charity, it is the same as if he possessed many lamps and torches without oil. If you light a lamp or torch with no oil, it can smoke and give a bad odor, but it cannot produce light. Similarly, one who possesses riches without charity can burn with anger or smoke with pride or have the foul odor of avarice; without charity, it is utterly impossible to produce light.[13]

Caesarius also treats charity as a giver of several gifts.

> Drink to the thirsty, food to the hungry, pleasure for those placed in bitterness, true and acceptable consolation for the sad, a haven for those who are wavering, a path for the erring, a country for strangers.[14]

Baldwin of Ford, Archbishop of Canterbury (1120–1190)

Baldwin was a Cistercian and a contemplative. His preaching is cross-referenced with multiple texts and a love of medieval categorizing. He is capable of using excellent images and finely arguing them. "Tractate XIV, On the Order of Charity,"[15] was delivered in Latin to a monastic congregation and stems from the time of Baldwin's work as abbot of Ford. It is filled with philosophical and patristic borrowings and allusions.

The sermon begins with the interesting proposal, based on Song of Songs 2:4–5, that love is an affliction. The "bride" and her turmoil related to charity is a description of the monastic soul seeking God.

Baldwin starts the sermon by reasoning from the lesser to the greater, describing forms of human loving prior to speaking of God's love: natural, social, conjugal, incestuous, and other impure loves, vain love, and holy love. In describing this latter love, Baldwin asks, "But if the love of God is charity and charity is virtue and strength, the greatest strength of all, how can the love of God be an affliction?"[16] This paradox is answered by the description of the soul's desire for God as that which is both thwarted and fulfilled.

Baldwin defines the relationships among charity, love, and virtues and then describes the ordering of virtue for daily life. "Charity is set in order by evaluation, by zeal, and by choice."[17]

Some of the ordering work of charity includes ordering the work of the angels, the mystery of our redemption, the subjecting of everything to God. Baldwin notes that, "When charity has been set in order and when it has ordered [everything else] in whatever way it has ordered it, then everything else is likewise set in order. [Charity] is itself the order of the things it regulates, and nothing which is done in charity can be out of order."[18]

Baldwin's sermon is unusual in its sophistication. What is so interesting about this use of the Song of Song texts as a backdrop for preaching on love/charity is that the sermon implicitly points out that true charity is always at one remove for attainment, that is, the longing of the soul for perfected love is always an open question and invitation. In other words, charity's ordering is always in process.

Saint Bernard (1091–1153)

Saint Bernard gave this sermon for the Feast of Saint Andrew. The text listed is from 1 Corinthians 13: "Charity is patient, is kind…Charity never falleth away."[19] The audience for the text is a monastic community. Bernard's intention is to celebrate the martyrdom of Saint Andrew and show how his life and death exemplify the type of love of which Paul writes.

Bernard's intention is also formed by the influences of mysticism, which emerges in some lyrical meditations within the sermon. Two of these are on the cross and the description of the faithful as fish. By way of paradox and contrast, Bernard says of the cross: "But what wonder is it that He Who imparted sweetness to raging fire imparted the same to the wood of the cross? Or how can the cross seem bitter when the very fire is found possessed of so sweet a savour?"[20] The "fish" are the faithful who are "enclosed in the apostolic net."[21]

Bernard develops this sermon through multiple quotes from the scripture and comparisons at several points between the crucifixions of Andrew and Jesus. The sensuous and lyrical descriptions of Jesus' humanity and sufferings as the Lord of love are richly descriptive and conflicted through Bernard's use of paradoxes: "Thy fears fortify us, Thy sadness rejoice us, They weariness refresh us, Thy agitation calm us, Thy desolation console us."[22] The content of the entire sermon is a nonlinear description of salvation history. The imagery is associative and cumulative rather than strictly logical in development.

Near the end of the sermon Bernard personifies faith, hope, and love:

> Says patience, urged on by fear, "I am constrained to act in this wise"; says the good will attracted by the motive of hope, "To act in this wise is expedient and necessary for me"; but charity, inflamed by the Holy Spirit, knows nothing of constraint or expediency; she says, "I will, I desire, I am full of eager longing to act in this wise." You observe how much subliminity, how much security, how much of sweetness there is in charity.[23]

The major language strategy of this sermon is the overall urging of Bernard to his listeners to meditate. "Let us mount, therefore, with the two feet of meditation and prayer."[24]

His sermon offers to the contemporary preacher the possibility of exploring the dynamics of love in 1 Corinthians 13 through a sermon rich in images of love, based on biblical passages, or actually employing good guided imagery as part of the sermon and/or the worship service.

John Wycliffe (1324–1384)

John Wycliffe's audience is indeterminate from a reading of this sermon except inasmuch as he perceives them to be susceptible to sects of their day. The sermon is a model of adherence to and explanation of each verse of this chapter. He sums up the direction of his sermon in the first sentence: "In this chapter Paul tells how men should know charity, and how men should keep charity; and this knowledge is much needed by every member of the holy church."[25]

Wycliffe calls the descriptions of love "conditions" and says "Look at these conditions, and decide whether you have them all in you; and if you do not have them, bestir yourself to have them all whole."[26]

As with Augustine's sermon, Wycliffe also speaks as the reformer and polemicist (though in gentler tones). Part of his intended audience and target is what he calls "the four sects" or the four orders of friars who were abusing the faithful in spiritual and material terms. It would be an interesting exercise to ask a contemporary preacher which groups she or he would target today in the same manner. Wycliffe uses the 1 Corinthians text as a form of pastoral admonition against the forces of heresy within the church.

Saint Thomas Aquinas (1379–1471)

No sermons of Saint Thomas Aquinas are available in English translation. However, a compendium of preaching resources was made available for Roman Catholic priests who preach. The older homiletical resources in any tradition, including this one, tend to be rich in historical materials for use in preaching.

Sections of this four-volume work include a variety of traditional quotes and views from different parts of the Catholic tradition, including biblical, exegetical, moral, the Church Fathers, liturgical, theological, hagiographical, and papal commentary of one sort or another.

In commenting on the texts for Quinquagesima Sunday, the entire chapter of 1 Corinthians 13 is included as the epistle reading for the Sunday. A summary of Aquinas' views for the preacher include these:

- Charity consists in the love of God as the object of our eternal happiness…The neighbor is the secondary object of charity, and he is loved for God's sake.
- Charity implies true friendship…God communicates to us his own eternal happiness, and the love which is founded on this exchange of gifts is true friendship.
- Charity does not pass away, as do the other theological virtues. "There is no comparison between the perfection of charity in this life and in the next; for, no matter how great our degree of charity here below, it can never equal the charity we have in heaven."
- Our grade of charity will depend on the will of God for each individual. It does not depend on any natural inclination of ours. "The Holy Spirit distributes his gifts as he pleases…At the same time, it can be increased…by a deeper rooting of charity in the subject."
- Charity "is the root and foundation of the other virtues, because they feed on charity and without it they are dead; it is their mother, because the others are born of our desire for the love of God, which is charity."[27]

John Calvin (1509–1564)

John Calvin was the sixteenth century's premier Reformed theologian. Records show that he produced numerous sermons on 1 Corinthians 13. However, according to Calvin archival reporting in this country[28] an ambitious librarian in the 1800s was cleaning library shelves and threw out the sermons. No English translations of any sermons on 1 Corinthians 13 are available. Calvin's biblical commentary on that chapter, however, is noteworthy for its use of languages and translations and some of its pithy observations, one of which will suffice here:

> *Whether knowledge, it will be destroyed.* We have already seen the meaning of these words; but from this arises a

question of no small importance—whether those who in this world excel either in learning, or in other gifts, will be on a level with idiots in the kingdom of God? In the *first* place, I should wish to admonish pious readers, not to harass themselves more than is meet in the investigation of these things...for the Lord himself has, by his silence, called us back from such curiosity.[29]

Nikolaus Ludwig von Zinzendorf (1700–1760)

Count Nikolaus Ludwig von Zinzendorf is associated with Moravian theology and ecclesiology. His writings and thought brought a unique stamp to the Protestant faith of his time. In the Brethren Chapel in London on September 11, 1746, Zinzendorf preached on 1 Corinthians 13:2, "And if I have prophetic powers, and understand all mysteries and all knowledge, and if I have all faith, so as to remove mountains, but do not have love, I gain nothing."

Zinzendorf plays the power of cognitive knowledge against the experience of God's love, the latter being the only thing of true importance and the former sometimes preventing a true experience of God. "I am so crammed with false principles that I cannot find my way into order and simplicity; I am preoccupied in opposition to the Savior!"[30] The sermon is undoubtedly pitched to the affective responses of the listener through a series of christological images, hymn verses, and an oddly contrasting form of almost scientific descriptions of life and knowledge.

> O dear friends, do not imagine that we know the Savior; we begin to know Him only when we have loved Him very tenderly, when we have loved Him first above all things, when for us nothing more in the world is in competition with Him, when we have forgotten ourselves on account of Him, our health, our life, our possessions and goods.[31]

Zinzendorf goes on to describe how recognizing the love of God comes through the agency of the Holy Spirit.

> One is never converted by a preacher, never leaves a sermon in a blessed state, if one did not come into the

church already awakened...it is nevertheless never the responsibility of the preacher that one is awakened, but rather the Holy Spirit acted at least a minute, an instant, before a word touched me, before words fall into my heart, before a sentence, a paragraph, a conclusion, a proposition becomes my text, my principle...It is not the conception; it is not the birth; rather, it is the first food of the living heart...for He Himself is the main food and drink.[32]

The mystical language of unity with Christ that Zinzendorf employs describes the creature who experiences God's love in this way: "I believe that there is a point in time when God my Creator Jesus Christ will marry me in body and soul, this poor creature, His poor human creature, His little worm, His poor little soul, and fetch me home."[33]

Zinzendorf's use of Christ-mysticism and imagery is significant throughout the sermon as the focal point for the person seeking to know God's love. The anthropology of the sermon depicts the human being as passive before God, awaiting the Holy Spirit's touch to understand the true nature of love incarnate. Zinzendorf gives the 1 Corinthians 13 chapter an explicit christocentric interpretation that the words of the chapter themselves do not contain. He concludes:

> If something brings a man out of consternation and restlessness into freedom, into contentment, and the Saviour does not come into the heart at the same time, the Crucified One does not move into the mind at the same time, He does not stand with the opened side before the heart, and this peace and reassurance do not arise from a view of the wounds, from touching the marks of the nails, from the pierced side, but rather from some other, even the best quarter, then it is a perdition and misfortune for the poor human creature.[34]

Jonathan Edwards (1703–1758)

Jonathan Edwards' lucid, thoughtful proclamation is displayed in a sermon on 1 Corinthians 13:1–3 entitled

"Christian Love As Manifested In The Heart And Life."[35] Date and place of delivery are not specified. Edwards' sermon is a marvel of the typical Puritan sermonic form of text–doctrine–application. The sermon could easily be titled "An Anatomy of Love." Reading the sermon is akin to the experience of examining a multifaceted rare gem. Edwards begins with a definition of charity and describes it as the source for all other types and kinds of love. From there he approaches the theme from multiple perspectives.

Anyone preaching a series on 1 Corinthians 13 would find a significant source of ideas available in this sermon. For example, in one category, Edwards describes the various *types of people* one should love: "We are to do good both to the *good* and to the *bad*";[36] "We should do good both to *friends* and *enemies*";[37] "We should do good both to the *thankful* and the *unthankful.*"[38]

In another category, he describes the *manner or mode* in which one should do good to others: "That our doing good *be not in a mercenary spirit,*"[39] "That our doing good be free, it is requisite that we do it *cheerfully* or *heartily*";[40] "That we do it *liberally and bountifully.*"[41]

As Edwards logically develops this anatomy of love, he emerges with some interesting specifications and conclusions that are only *implicit* in the text. His argument is a form of posing opposites. He notes that envy, a censorious spirit, anger, and harsh judgments of others form the opposite mode of loving them.

Edwards concludes by asking questions of his listeners as they attempt to apply his preaching to their lives. The questions fix on what he calls "holy practice." "If you can honestly meet these tests, then you have the evidence that your grace is of the kind that tends to holy practice, and to growth in it. And though you may fall, through God's mercy you shall rise again."[42]

Edwards' preaching recommends it to contemporary proclamation that occasionally wishes to use language strategies focusing on the specifically didactic and deductive form of sermon.

From the Eighteenth Century to the Twenty-First Century

Wider printing of books and pamphlets, increased literacy, and publications of sermonic materials in Europe and America from the eighteenth century to the present offer more evidence of proclamation on 1 Corinthians 13. The preachers and their topics from this era must also be read for what is not present. With the advent of printed sermons by laity, women, and persons of color, what sermons are available show that the themes they addressed emerged primarily out of Old and New Testament texts focused on the person of Jesus, justice, and community.

John M. Wesley (1703–1791)

John Wesley's sermon is fascinating for its initial address related to the translation of the word *love*. Wesley traces the loss of *agape* to its mistranslation as *charity* in the works of Roger Daniel and John Field, printers to the English parliament in 1649. Wesley notes: "Thousands of these [common men and women] are misled thereby, and imagine that the charity treated of in this chapter refers chiefly, if not wholly, to outward actions, and to mean little more than almsgiving!"[43] He also takes issue with other mistranslations of the text.

The sermon is arranged around an "is/is not" pattern with a resolution. His outline reads:

I. What the charity here spoken of is;

II. What those things are which are usually put in the place of it. We may then,

III. Observe, that neither of them, nor all of them put together, can supply it.[44]

Wesley describes the process of arriving at the meaning of true love.

> What a beautiful gradation there is, each step rising above the other, in the enumeration of those several things, which some or other of those that are called Christians, and are usually accounted so, really believe will supply the absence of love. St. Paul begins at the

lowest point, *talking well,* and advances step by step...A step above eloquence is knowledge; faith is a step above this. Good works are a step above faith: and even above this, is suffering for righteousness' sake. Nothing is higher than this, but Christian love: the love of our neighbour, flowing from the love of God.[45]

Wesley also challenges his listeners as Methodists who focus on the "lesser" doctrines of the faith as a substitute for true Christian love: "You constantly speak of salvation...You maintain that a man is justified by faith...You insist...we are saved by faith...We are of all men most inexcusable...while we indulge any of these [holy] tempers."[46]

George Whitefield (1714–1770)

George Whitefield was, like Wesley, a great revivalist who worked both in England and in America. His sermon "The Great Duty of Charity Recommended,"[47] focuses on 1 Corinthians 13:8, which he translates as "Charity never faileth." The sermon interprets charity as "the grace of love"[48] in two ways: first, as actual almsgiving and then as care and concern for the souls of others.

Whitefield's particular target is clergy and the wealthy who refuse to do either. "Let me beseech you to consider, which will stand you best at the day of judgment, so much more money expended at a horse-race, or a cockpit, at a play or masquerade, or so much given for the relief of your fellow-creatures, and for the distressed members of Jesus Christ."[49] Whitefield is particularly pointed in his remarks to clergy:

> Our clergy...are only seeking after preferment, running up and down, to obtain one benefice after another; and to heap up an estate, either to spend on the pleasures of life, or to gratify their sensual appetites, while the poor of their flock are forgotten; nay, worse, they are scorned, hated, and disdained.[50]

Whitefield concludes, "But you cannot be true Christians without having charity to your fellow-creatures, be they friends or enemies, if in distress. And, therefore, exert yourselves in this duty, as is commanded by the blessed Jesus: and if you have true charity, you shall live and reign with him for ever."[51]

Rev. H. P. Liddon (1829-1890)

Rev. H. P. Liddon was the Canon of Saint Paul's, in London, England. Liddon published heavily in the area of preaching. In December 1879 he offered an Advent sermon in Saint Paul's Cathedral entitled "The First Five Minutes After Death,"[52] which is based on 1 Corinthians 13:12 (KJV): "Then shall I know even as also I am known." The sermon is a fascinating set of speculations about what life after death will be like. Liddon proposes life after death as the soul alive without a body, as a spiritual progression, and as an entry into the presence of God.

> Not merely will the scene be new, and to us, as yet, unimaginable–not merely will the beings around us be new–the shapes, the forms, the conditions of being, strange, and, as yet, wholly inconceivable, but we ourselves shall have undergone a change–a change so complete that we cannot here and now anticipate its full meaning.[53]

Liddon's means of applying the laws of faith for the listener come in the form of these assertions:

> Moral evil will be buried with the decaying body in the grave, while the soul escapes, purified by the separation from its grosser companion, to the regions of holiness and grace. Surely, brethren, this is an illusion which will not stand the test...And there is no reasonable ground for thinking that at death the influences of a whole lifetime will cease to operate upon the character...Why, I ask, should death have this result?[54]

The conclusion of the sermon then invites the faithful to consider their impending deaths with the preacher's plea voiced through an echoing of the Nicene Creed:

> That first five minutes–that first awakening to a new existence, with its infinite possibilities–will only be

tolerable if we have indeed, with the hands of faith and love, laid on the hope set before us in the person of Jesus Christ our Lord and Savior, Who for us men and for our salvation took flesh and was crucified, and rose from the dead, and ascended into heaven, and has pleaded and is pleading now...for us, the weak and erring children of the fall.[55]

Unnamed Lutheran Pastor from the 19th Century

The eschatological ending of 1 Corinthians 13 is addressed again through the reality of death as an occasion for a sermon by an anonymous Lutheran pastor in late nineteenth-century America. His text is 1 Corinthians 13:13. The sermon is couched in the midst of a second tragedy: "We wept here two years ago at the bier of the pastor's wife...We have come here today to weep at the bier of the pastor's only child. The parsonage is now stripped of the last earthly element of joy to its lone occupant."[56]

The sermon is divided into three sections with the pastor using the triad of faith, hope, and charity as a means of calling the bereaved to a new life. "Faith yields you its kindly office, dear father, in this hour of sadness...It reminds you that this child of yours is embraced in the eternal counsels of Divine Mercy."[57]

"Hope will go out with us to God's Acre and lay a wreath of Forget-me-nots–all the promises of our dear Lord–upon your child's grave, to rouse your faltering spirit whenever you visit it."[58] And, concludes the preacher, "Love, then, my dear friend, will teach you to say in this hour of grief: 'Lord, gladly do I commit to Thy hands what Thou lovest so much better than I'...God has picked you for a jewel in the Redeemer's crown."[59]

Phillips Brooks (1835–1893)

Phillips Brooks was one of the best known of America's nineteenth-century preachers. An Episcopalian bishop, Rector of Trinity Church in Boston, his preaching is simple, vivid, and tenderhearted. In his sermon "The Knowledge of God,"[60] Brooks preaches, in sequence and in connection, two texts:

John 10:15 (KJV), "As the Father knoweth me, even so know I the Father," and 1 Corinthians 13: 12 (KJV), "Then shall I know even as also I am known."

Brooks links the two texts by developing the first one in terms of the intimate relationships within the Trinity and the Corinthians verse: "What Christ was we shall be some day, and because we shall be it some day, we may begin to be it now...you and God, one system of power knit together in mutual knowledge, and in common standards!"[61]

Brooks also talks about the artificial separation of our knowing and our obeying God and says that the text means "the promise that we shall know includes the promise that we shall obey!...I hear...the ringing of the hammers on the anvils where in the fire of the love of God the perfect obedience of His redeemed is forging his perfect will into the instruments of perfect deeds."[62]

Henry Drummond (1851–1897)

Henry Drummond, a nineteenth-century Scottish preacher, writes in simple, short sentences to describe what love is and is not. His sermon is called "The Greatest Thing in the World."[63] Neither the date nor audience is specified, though the language of the sermon would imply a congregation of everyday laity.

Drummond follows Paul's own outline: "We may divide it [the chapter] into three parts. In the beginning of the short chapter, we have love contrasted; in the heart of it, we have love analyzed; toward the end, we have love defended as the supreme gift."[64] Drummond uses an interesting metaphor to describe what he calls the "spectrum of love."

> So Paul passes this thing, love, through the magnificent prism of his inspired intellect and it comes out on the other side broken up into its elements...Will you observe what its elements are? Will you notice that they have common names; that they are virtues which we hear about every day, that they are things which can be practiced by every man in every place in life...the spectrum of love has nine ingredients: Patience ...Sincerity.[65]

Drummond has a knack for aphoristic language. A single sentence could serve today's proclaimer as a sermonic intention and/or sermon title. For example, he draws a useful distinction between charity and love: "Charity is only a little bit of love, and there may be even be, and there is, a great deal of charity without love."[66] His description of giving money to beggars as an act of charity and not love is chilling and contemporaneous with all times and places.

The latter part of the sermon uses the figure of Christ as the ultimate instigator and teacher of love. "Stand before that mirror, reflect Christ's character, and you will be changed into the same image from tenderness to tenderness."[67] His accumulation of phrases related to Christ provides a concluding form of *imitatio Christi* as a means of applying the text to daily life.

He concludes by noting that withholding love means Christ's death was in vain: "It means that He suggested nothing at all in our thoughts, that He inspired nothing in all our lives, that we were not once near enough to Him to be seized with the spell of His compassion for the world."[68]

Drummond's sermon models pastoral care, compassion, simplicity of language, and effective uses of daily examples from life in illustrating this chapter on love.

John Henry Newman (1801–1890)

John Henry Newman's sermon, "The Centrality of Charity"[69] is rendered in the elegant language of an Oxford don with a deep insight into the human heart. Neither audience nor date is specified with these sermons.

Newman makes use of a *via negativa* in describing how true Christian love falls short and therefore the manifestations and indications of what it is not. Like Jonathan Edwards, he offers an anatomy of love, though in the negative. His insights are significant. Most humans sadly love from law and fear motives as they understand their religion. "It is possible to obey, not from love towards God and man, but from a sort of conscientiousness short of love; from some notion of acting up to a law."[70] Some love minus any religious aspect, and that too falls short.

Newman strikes at the core of the problem when he notes: "Without love there may be remorse, regret, self-reproach, self-condemnation, but there is not saving penitence. There may be conviction of the reason, but not conversion of the heart."[71] One of the more modern notes Newman sounds is how increasing amounts of stimulation from the world around us are needed if we do not love.

> Why is it that we are looking out for novelties? Why is it that we complain of want of variety in a religious life?…Why is it that lowly duties, such as condescending to men of low estate, are distasteful and irksome? Why is it that we need powerful preaching, or interesting and touching books, in order to keep our thoughts on God? Why is it that our faith is so dispirited and weakened by hearing casual objections urged against the doctrine of Christ?[72]

All this Newman ascribes to "our proneness to be taken up and engrossed with trifles."[73] The conclusion of the sermon offers the summary insight that we have an abundance of too many things and thus lose sight of love. The remedy? Newman provides a powerful mediation on the cross.

> Think of the cross when you rise and when you lie down, when you go out and when you come in, when you eat and when you walk and when you converse, when you buy and when you sell, when you labor and when you rest, consecrating and sealing all your doings with this one mental action, the thought of the Crucified. Do not talk of it to others, be silent, like the penitent woman, who showed her love in deep subdued acts.[74]

The tone of this sermon offers suggestions for today's preacher offering homilies during the Lenten season.

Henry Ward Beecher (1813–1887)

One of Henry Ward Beecher's sermons on this text was delivered on October 22, 1871, and entitled "Sovereignty and Permanence of Love." Beecher's intention was to discuss love in a variety of daily ways and to exhort listeners to loving action.

Voices from the Historical Pulpit 61

The sermon, like much of Beecher's work is very "practical" in nature. Biblical text is quoted periodically but not in sequence, and the theological arguments are derived from Beecher's observations about the nature of people.

Typical of his time, Beecher depends on *ethical* language as his major perspective in speaking of love, with repeated phrases such as "sympathy," "sympathetic benevolence," and "Christian character." The modern-day preacher may consider the differences between theological and ethical approaches to this text.

Like Drummond, Beecher uses simple language, and some sentences can provide suggestions for a single sermon in and of themselves. For example, "Love wrings tears; love shuts up men; love chastises men; love grasps men even unto death. In some sense love may be said to remorseless."[75]

G. H. Morrison (n. d. – 19th/20th centuries)

G. H. Morrison was a Scottish preacher from Glasgow. His sermon on 1 Corinthians 13[76] is limited to a single phrase, "Now I know in part" (1 Corinthians 13:12a). The sermon does not keep to the text, but its charm lies in the focus on the *mystery* of life and faith as exemplified in the life, words, and deeds of Jesus Christ.

> Things never become less mysterious, always more, when they have passed through the mind and heart of Jesus Christ...Jesus enlarged the mystery of things, intensified it, deepened it twentyfold...And, then when common actions are irradiated, and common lives flash into moral glories, when the mysteries of life, and love, and death, and God, so baffle us that we can only say with Paul "we know in part"–we shall be nearer the spirit of Jesus than we dreamed.[77]

Harry Emerson Fosdick (1878–1969)

Harry Emerson Fosdick's sermon, "The Most Durable Power in the World,"[78] focuses on a single phrase, "Love never faileth!" The sermon is set in the social context of the earlier half of the twentieth century. Fosdick makes four points regarding his chosen phrase: "Love does not fail in so far as man always has to come back to it when he wants something constructive done."[79] Second, "love does not fail in so far as it creates a standard of judgment by which anything less than itself is shown up as inferior."[80] Third, "love does not fail in so far as it makes beautiful the personal lives of those who exercise it."[81] And finally, "love does not fail in so far as it keeps discovering possibilities, both personal and social, among the actualities, and brings them out."[82]

Fosdick chooses an interpretation of love that matches his doctrine of preaching a socially contextualized gospel.

> We habitually think of love as emotional. We have an unruly *penchant* for interpreting it in sentimental terms. But love is cognitive. By it alone can some truths be discerned. It only has eyes to see some realms of knowledge...There are truths about humanity that never would have been known unless love had discovered them.[83]

Perhaps the most interesting line in the sermon related to the meaning and context of love is in the conclusion, in Fosdick's cry, "Ah, Cross of Christ, grow real to us again."[84]

George Hodges (1856–1919)

George Hodges was Dean of the Episcopal Theological School, Cambridge, Massachusetts. Hodges' sermon is typical of an early era, in which the translation of love from the Greek was rendered as *charity*. The sermon is also somewhat noteworthy for its grumpy tone; is it possible that the subject matter was making itself felt in Hodges' own ministry? or that he is preaching during Lent?

He discerns that "between the common notion of charity and the sense in which St. Paul used the word, there is an antagonistic difference."[85] Hodges applies the word *charity* in a rather interesting way by noting its manifestations in human discourse: "The particular kind of speech which St. Paul has immediately in mind here is ecclesiastical speech: that is, he is thinking of the things that are said in church and in connection with the church."[86] Hodges unfolds numerous examples from church history and concludes: "All of this uncharitable controversy,–and unchristian because uncharitable,–shows how true Christianity is to the facts of human nature."[87]

Hodges concludes:

> I have thus dealt with charity as an element in ecclesiastical speech, partly because that is what St. Paul had especially in mind, and partly because it is easier to speak of the faults of controversy than of the faults of conversation. But you see how it all applies to social speech. You see how it touches all or comments on our neighbors…Now Lent begins…Shall we not turn…To the regulation of our speech, to the suppression of all unfraternal comment, to the better cultivation of the grace of charity.[88]

John Henry Jowett (1863–1923)

John Henry Jowett served as both a Congregational and Presbyterian minister in England and in America. His sermon "The Modesty of Love"[89] is based on 1 Corinthians 13:4, 5 and deals with the topics of envy and misbehavior. The sermon is written in very simple language, and many sentences can stand on their own as proverbs or sermon titles.

The sermon addresses each of the verses with such statements as these: "There is only one thing that can kill envy, and that is love…If you want to destroy the envy that is lurking in your heart, you must have created in your heart the atmosphere of love, and the secret of that atmosphere you can learn at the foot of the Cross."[90]

Jowett points out contradictions in this way. "No man has a right to be blunt in his speech and shapeless and ugly in his behavior whatever may be the worth and rectitude of his meaning."[91]

The sermon ends with a depiction of personified love.

> If love had a right to the uppermost seat at a feast, and somebody else has got it, love would seek not her own, but would gratefully insist on the rights of the other. If

love had a sitting in the Church of Christ and came and found that someone else was seated there, love would not behave itself unseemly; love would seek not her own, but would cheerfully seek a seat elsewhere. Is this not the way of love? Would not this be the way of Christ?[92]

George Arthur Buttrick (1892–1980)

George Buttrick was the famed preacher of Madison Avenue Presbyterian Church in the early decades of the twentieth century. In his sermon "Knowledge and Love,"[93] Buttrick focuses on 1 Corinthians 12–14 and addresses the issue of what it means to be an agnostic. After building a case for the general agnostic view of life, he compares it to that of a Christian agnostic: "The difference between agnosticism and biblical agnosticism is that the one says, 'in a mirror darkly,' while the Bible adds, 'but we see.'"[94]

In a carefully argued manner, Buttrick then notes two other things: "Another item regarding our broken knowledge; we know it is broken."[95] And then, "we must trade bravely on our partial knowledge and on the deeper knowledge of our ignorance, for we must go on living."[96] For Buttrick these statements add up to faith: "We must make our venture."[97]

Of the Christian's faith, he says: "Faith confronts three facts: one, we see in a mirror: two, we do see; and three, we must live and die."[98] He then moves on to hope, which is "our knowledge of our ignorance, the eternity from which we see the limits of time."[99]

Buttrick then identifies Christ as the center that holds this all together, and returns to a comment on seeing through a mirror darkly. "The old maps had captions over areas not yet explored: 'Here be dragons,' or 'Here be demons,' or 'Here be sirens.' Sir John Franklin wrote instead, 'Here is God,' and so made his brave ventures."[100]

Karl Barth (1886–1968)

The famed Reformed theologian Karl Barth wrote on preaching, and some of his sermons have been translated into

English. There is no English translation for a sermon on 1 Corinthians 13. However, in a 1970 edition of his *Church Dogmatics,* the final volume contains what are called "Aids for the Preacher." While not sermons, homilies, or even "postils," The assignment of 1 Corinthians 13 to Quinquagesima Sunday notes four pertinent sections of Barth's *Church Dogmatics* that pertain to the passage's theology. One of these sections notes:

> [Love]...is the future eternal light shining in the present. It therefore needs no change of form. It is that which continues...Already, then, love is the eternal activity of the Christian. This is the reason why love abides. This is the reason why to say this is to say the final and supreme thing about it. This is the reason why we had to say previously that it is love alone that counts (vv. 1–3) and love alone that conquers (vv. 4–7). This is the reason why it is *the* way.[101]

William Edwin Sangster (1900–1960)

William Edwin Sangster was a Methodist preacher from Great Britain. His sermon "When Hope is Dead–Hope On!" is based on the interplay of two biblical texts: 1 Corinthians 13:13 and Hebrews 6:19.[102] The background of the sermon is pre–World War II London, and it was preached to his London parishioners.

The sermon draws out the differences between secular hope–which he calls optimism–and the hope grounded in God. The preacher uses a variety of everyday examples to point to evidences of humanity's often-unwarranted sense of optimism. Sangster says: "We go forward into this dark period in our nation's life, not inflated with foolish optimism which seems to give buoyancy to those who do not know Christ, but with a quiet unquenchable hope drawn from the deep sources of our faith."[103] According to Sangster, Christian hope is based on the indestructibility of truth and the knowledge that God is on the throne.

What makes this sermon focus on hope in such a compelling manner is the implied urgency about the country's approach to war. Sangster's sermon is a significant pastoral, contextualized response to one point of Paul's chapter in the interests of context.

Karl Rahner (1904–1984)

Karl Rahner offers a sermon on 1 Corinthians from its place in the lectionary: Fourth Sunday in Ordinary Time (Year C), entitled "A Thing that Is Transparent Must Be Empty."[104] Rahner's intention in this short homily form is to "consider the relationship between knowledge and love."[105] The sermon covers the sections of Paul's text methodically and occasionally adds some startling insights related to this relationship. These include knowledge, the role of truth, mystery, and incomprehensibility.

> Indeed, if we examine our text with care, we shall see something which is generally overlooked or misinterpreted: Paul means that even in the consummation to come knowledge is perfected only when it is done away with, so to speak; when it abandons itself, so to speak, in love.[106]

Rahner's sermon invites the modern preacher to reflect on how this sermon can be preached in a lectionary context and how that is related to the liturgical season of Epiphany with one of its themes as enlightenment in Christ.

Walter J. Burghardt, S.J. (Contemporary)

Walter Burghardt's preaching, regardless of theme, is known for the much-spoofed "three points sermon." He is, however, a master of the form. One of the homilies he preached at a wedding is entitled "You Have Ravished My Heart."[107]

The sermon's three sections are each devoted to three texts the couple chose: Song of Songs 4:8–16; 1 Corinthians 12:31–13:8a and Matthew 22:35–40. Burghardt moves in ascending fashion theologically through each text to glean the insights they yield on love. Through the use of accumulation–theologically and by examples and text–he builds his case for what Christian love is. These three sections could be defined variously as the creation, definition, and all-encompassing views of love or the wisdom, poetry, and glory of love.

Burghardt describes the link between God and humanity in terms of incarnation:

> The God who shaped you in His likeness, the God who brought you together against all odds, this same God lives within you. And wonder of wonders, this loving Father's only Son, who bloodied a cross to link you like this in love, will soon nestle in your palms, cradle on your tongues, home in your hearts. Such is the love that pervades you today.[108]

This homily links Jesus' "Great Commandment" with Paul's epistle. Burghardt's homiletical style is intimate, liberally laced with contemporary illustrations, and uses text in both a historical and imagistic fashion.

Robert Edward Luccock (late 20th century)

Robert Edward Luccock's sermon is written around two texts: Matthew 5:39 and 1 Corinthians 13:7–8. Luccock combines patient acceptance and suffering of others with the endurance of love as the sermon's dual themes and uses Tolstoy's story "God Sees the Truth But Waits," and the example of marital reconciliation from Eugene O'Neill's "Days Without End" to illustrate much of the sermon. Says Luccock, "In the face of love's final word neither principalities nor powers will be able to separate you from the love of God."[109]

Paul Tillich (1886–1965)

From Paul Tillich's pulpit at Union Theological Seminary he, like Rahner, picks up on the relationship of knowledge to love in a sermon on 1 Corinthians 13: 8–12 entitled "Knowledge Through Love."[110]

Tillich's sermon is from the existential school. If one word describes the sermon—a word used repeatedly by Tillich—it is *fragmentary*. Tillich examines the variety of ways our knowledge is perpetually fragmentary. In fact, the sermon in its very form remains fragmentary purposefully. The ending provides only a provisional sense of resolution:

> Man is a fragment and a riddle to himself...Paul experienced the breakdown of a system of life and

thought which he believed to be a whole, a perfect truth without riddle or gaps. He then found himself buried under the pieces of his knowledge and his morals. But Paul never tried again to build up a new, comfortable house out of the pieces. He dwelt with the pieces. He realized always that fragments remain fragments.[111]

Tillich's existential style is not for everyone, but he does speak of and to the human condition in a realistic manner.

Fleming Rutledge (Contemporary)

Fleming Rutledge is an Episcopalian priest, and for Trinity Church in Boston she offered this sermon on the last Sunday after the Epiphany, combining 1 Corinthians 13:7–8 and Luke 9:28–31–an account of the Transfiguration.[112] The sermon begins with news accounts of love gone wrong. She then shows how a misunderstanding of love wants to maintain a transfiguration "mountain high."

Rutledge describes how true love "comes down," whether that is helping someone felled by a car accident, Martin Luther King, Jr.'s, going down to Memphis (and to his death), or Jesus' coming down from the mountain:

> [Jesus] He comes down from the mountain; he comes down from the throne of the majesty on high; he comes down from the infinite spaces of uncreated light and prepares to enter the darkness of human suffering and human pain. God is not looking down with detachment from a great distance...he reaches out, he comes down, to seek *you,* to find *you,* to embrace *you.* The love Olympics have gone to Jerusalem.[113]

Martin Luther King, Jr. (1929–1968)

A collection of Martin Luther King, Jr.'s, sermons emerged from his preaching at Dexter Avenue Baptist Church during and after the bus protest in Montgomery, Alabama. One of the more remarkable sermons is a fictional epistle from Saint Paul to the American people. In a preface King notes that when he received the letter, he spent a great deal of time translating the

Greek. He says: "If the content of this epistle sounds strangely Kingian instead of Paulinian, attribute it to my lack of complete objectivity rather than Paul's lack of clarity."[114]

The sermon contains critiques of the system of capitalism and the segregation both of society and church. While King uses a variety of Pauline texts, he concludes with verses from 1 Corinthians 13.

> But even more, Americans, you may give your goods to feed the poor, you may bestow great gifts to charity, and you may tower high in philanthropy, but if you have not love, your charity means nothing…You must come to see that a man may be self-centered in his self-denial and self-righteous in his self-sacrifice. His generosity may feed his ego and his piety his pride…The greatest of all virtues is love. Here we find the true meaning of the Christian faith and of the cross. Calvary is a telescope through which we look into the long vista of eternity and see the love of God breaking into time.[115]

CHAPTER 4

Contemporary Sermons on 1 Corinthians 13

This chapter includes thirty-two contemporary sermons on 1 Corinthians 13. Women and men who are variously pastors, seminary instructors, evangelists, and theological students from a number of different faith perspectives share their faith through these sermons. Their work is presented in the areas of occasional sermon settings and the Revised Common Lectionary's appointment of the text in Year C, Fourth Sunday Epiphany.

These sermons are rich in resources for the reader. They are in a deep sense "homely," in that they emerged from the nitty-gritty, everydayness of the audiences before whom they were preached. For example, one sermon is preached on a feast day, another at a senior citizen center, a third as a basis for exploring the relationship between pastor and congregation, and another at the installation of a friend.

The writers suggest different structural and content perspectives. The variety of illustrations in these sermons contextualizes them, while some of them will travel well into other settings. Most importantly, these sermons demonstrate the wide variety of intentions that preachers can bring to the same text.

These sermons have been proclaimed before a multitude of audiences. The reader may decide how the sermons either follow or diverge from the commentary offered by the authors of this work, and how the reader's own homiletical style finds resonance in these texts.

Letting Love Loose

Charles L. Aaron, Jr.

I admit that I was naïve. I'll claim as my excuse the idealism of youth and the propaganda of seminary culture. They had kindled in me what had already been a spark: the desire for intellectual stimulation, new ideas, stretching my mind to its utmost and worshiping God with my mind. So when I saw the posters on campus advertising the debate about abortion, I knew I had to go. On one side was Phyllis Schlafly, on the other, a representative of NOW. I expected thoughtful, carefully reasoned discussions about the viability of fetuses, social and economic impacts, alternative methods of birth control, the delineation of the rights of the fetus, and the rights of the mother.

Expectations are not always fulfilled. What I got was a sideshow that would bring a tear of joy to the eye of a talk show host. Who could out-shout, out-applaud, out-hoot the other side? Who could spit out the nastiest, cleverest insults? Which side could drown out the other so that opinions could not be heard?

My expectations for this debate, even at a church-related university, may have been naïve—If my expectations were naïve, is it also naïve to cite Paul's words about love in the context of volatile debates? We are accustomed to hearing these words at weddings. We can see how Paul's words apply to the bride and groom. They will need patience and kindness to survive the stress of sharing their lives. For all its initial exuberance, marriage is a scary adventure, with more than enough opportunities to fall apart. How a couple love each other affects them, their children and families, and their community, so they need a love that "bears all things."

Can we pry Paul's words out of wedding ceremonies and let them be heard in the midst of debates about incendiary social and theological issues? Surely love is not too tender, too sweet to stand on its own in an auditorium swirling with anger. In the nearly twenty years since that debate on abortion, things have not gotten any quieter. The church universal and the United Methodist Church are being pulled nearly to the breaking point over issues like abortion and homosexuality, to name only two. So far, we have not been much inclined to hear Paul's words about love in the midst of these debates. The battle lines have been drawn; the other side is the enemy. Every General Conference turns out to be a teeth-clenching conflict. The intensity of the debate is certainly understandable. Lives are at stake; the witness of the church is at stake. Those who fight so hard may believe that they have no choice but to pump themselves up for battle. We need our best arguments, our best wisdom to defend those who need us. No whimpering plea to just get along is going to help. Neither will it do to say that the church should put these issues aside and get on with its "real business." The church, even from Paul's day, has debated important issues. Paul himself engaged in many disputes. We have to face the problems head on. Nevertheless, we must hear Paul as he writes here in 1 Corinthians.

Paul's words can help us because they were not directed to a beaming couple glowing with a love that doesn't know what's in store around the next bend in the road. They were written to a squabbling church. The Corinthian church bled from internal wounds. They fought over former pastors, sex, meat offered to idols, speaking in tongues, spiritual gifts, celebrating the Lord's supper. The members of the congregation came to the church from different backgrounds and socioeconomic strata. Their disagreements arose out of genuine attempts to understand their newfound faith in light of what they had known before. Their attempts to defend their positions had grown into spiritual pride. Their differences threatened to tear them apart. Paul is frustrated with their fighting and scolds them for their petulant disputes. From the beginning of the letter, Paul tells them to stop their bickering, not because it is unseemly and annoying, but because their unity in Christ is more fundamental than their differences.

Here in this chapter, Paul's description of love's qualities is a direct repudiation of the behavior of the Corinthians. Their actions are the opposite of love. They are jealous and quarrelsome (3:3), but love is not. They are boastful (3:21), but love is not. They are arrogant and proud (4:18–19), but love is not. They act shamefully (5:1–2), but love does not. Before the Corinthians can be a church, they must learn what love can do.[1] They can never address the substance of their disagreements until they discover that their unity in Christ is stronger than what separates them.

Can Paul's words, written to one congregation, help us in our vigorous debates about theology and social issues? Love may work well in a congregation, but is a denomination too large for love to do us any good? Does love even apply to these issues? The Corinthians did not seem to face problems that were beyond compromise, in which there was little if any middle ground, as we do. Either we will ordain homosexuals, or we will not. Either we will conduct same-gender ceremonies, or we will not. Either we will allow abortions in at least some circumstances, or we will not. Perhaps we have to look elsewhere for help.

Certainly we want the fighting to cease, but both sides may believe that the fighting cannot cease without one side winning, or without a schism. It is easy to look at someone else's fight and see how childish it seems. Much as a parent wants squawking kids to pipe down, so we want Christian groups to be able to get along. When we are in the middle of an argument, however, things don't look so simple, We argue because we have passionate feelings about the issues. We don't see ourselves as "insisting on our own way"; we see ourselves as "standing up for what we believe." We would even say that we take the positions we do because of love itself. We love the scriptures and do not want to see them misunderstood. We love people of same-gender orientation and don't want to see them oppressed. We love unwed mothers who have nowhere else to turn and want them to have options. We love unborn babies and want them to have a chance at life. How can we love people who threaten what is so important?

Paul would tell us that the basis for our unity is our relationship to Christ. We are the body of Christ, with each of us playing a part. As far as it goes, we would agree with those statements. How do we love people, though, even fellow Christians, who hold opinions that hurt people or seem to threaten the scriptures we cherish?

Paul, who has seen his share of church problems, places much trust in love to do things we might not expect it to do.

We can see that in a subtle shift in emphasis in Paul's words. In verses 1–3, Paul writes in first person: "If in the tongues of people I speak" [my translation]. Paul talks about our choice of having love to go with our prophetic powers, knowledge, and faith. The individual is in control of whether to choose love or not. In verses 4–7, however, Paul shifts to third person. Love itself becomes the subject of the sentence. "Love is patient, love is kind…love is not rude." Love does the hoping and believing. Paul's use of personification for love sounds almost as if love has a mind of its own. In verses 1–3 we have a choice about love, but in verses 4–7, love seems to kind of take over and do things on its own. Before we know it, this sweet, tender quality of love that we associate with puppies and babies and wedding bouquets starts to take charge. It begins to work within us to create new characteristics, transform our emotions, and burn away our weaknesses. If we let love in, we may find that we are no longer in control, that love is making us into people we didn't expect to become.

Love may not be able to change the real differences in perspective between opposing sides of big debates. We cannot issue a simplistic call to stop all the fussin' and fightin'. Nevertheless, Paul is willing to give love a lot of credit. Love believes all things and hopes all things. If we view our opponents as cynical and dangerous, love may believe in their good faith and willingness to listen. If we see no possibility for even civil exchange, love hopes for genuine sharing. Certainly, we need knowledge for our debates. We have to use our intellects to search out answers to complex questions of biblical exegesis and authority, as well as the results of scientific research. Paul is clear, though, that our knowledge is in part, and we see in a mirror dimly. If we have knowledge, but not love, we are nothing.

Let us be naïve enough to let love loose in our debates. Let us allow love to take control and show us things we cannot yet see. Let us allow love to melt away our childishness, name-calling and suspicion. Let us allow love to raise us above the quest to beat our opponent and join us together in the search for truth.

Interpreted by Love

Ronald J. Allen

Tired from a day of pumping the well for a sermon that wouldn't come, of dealing with the urgent issue of where the cap to the bottle of glue in the Bible School closet might be, and of wrestling with a committee in which it was difficult to find signs of life, but fortified by an adequate supply of popcorn, I settled into the late night movie.

The Last Picture Show. An appropriate title. Shot in black and white. The buildings in the one-street Texas town had that weathered, run-down look–paint peeling, shutters knocking in the wind, the grass rubbed away from the yard, leaving only bare ground.

One of the characters was Sonny, a high school boy who played guard on the football team and who got involved with his coach's wife. There was Ruth Popper, the coach's wife, a thin, plain-faced woman whose life has been as exciting as an empty paper bag until Sonny comes along. And Jacy, the rich girl who owns the town's only convertible, and who sleeps with whomever she needs to in order to be the center of attention.

Scene after scene of people saying, "Love me." Acting out their yearning in the back seats of cars, in creaky old beds, in cheap motel rooms, and yes, even on the back row of the last picture show in town.

It would be kind of funny if you didn't have the feeling that people around us–maybe even someone here–feels the same way. People saying, "Love me...love me...love me," but not knowing what love is or where to find it.

Just listen to the radio. I heard a song the other day admonishing undercover lovers to lie low. Years ago, I remember one lamenting that Lucille had picked a bad time to leave.

The Bible, of course, has its own love songs. One of them is 1 Corinthians 13. It's a long way, as we used to say, from Waylon, Willie, and the boys.

We usually hear 1 Corinthians 13 at weddings. A bride, her nervousness concealed by her long dress, and a knock-kneed groom, tuxedo pants a couple of sizes too small. Both of them quivering. They choke out the right words, and we all get misty-eyed as they march down the aisle into a new life.

When I was five, love was what I felt for an ice cream cone. When I was sixteen, love was goose bumps when I saw nearly anyone in a skirt. And in the church today, many of us think love is a warm, fuzzy feeling.

But for Paul, love is something else. It is the self-giving of one for another. "God proves [or shows] God's love for us in that while we were still sinners Christ died for us" (Rom. 5:8). And because of that, "God's love has been poured into our hearts through the Holy Spirit that has been given to us" (Rom. 5:5). Through the Holy Spirit, we can share that kind of love with one another.

Frederick Buechner, a Christian writer, captures this spirit. He calls Christian love something other than just an emotion. Christian love, for Buechner, is an act of will. Jesus never asks us to have warm, fuzzy feelings for our neighbors, but Jesus does tell us to be willing to work for our neighbors' well-being.

1 Corinthians 13 is about that kind of love–the love that God has for us and the love that we can have for another as a church. Paul doesn't so much define as describe it.

> If I speak in the tongues of mortals and of angels, but do not have love, I am a noisy gong or a clanging cymbal. And if I have prophetic powers, and understand all mysteries and all knowledge, and if I have all faith, so as to remove mountains, but do not have love, I am nothing. (vv. 1–3)

Paul begins by addressing the spiritual leaders in Corinth, those who had spoken in tongues. And he says to them, "You can be a member of the board and the President of the Congregation, have a string of perfect attendance pins for Bible School that reach from your shoulders to your knees, and be able to hold the congregation in the palm of your hand when you preach, but if you do not have love, you are about as valuable to the church as an already canceled check."

I can come to worship each week, sing the great hymns and praise choruses, be touched by the music, pray fervently, but if I never even learn the names of the persons sitting around me, how can I love them? And how can they love me?

People who love each other are patient and kind. So here is a question. How do you feel when someone growls at you? How do you feel when you growl at someone else? How do you feel when you snap at someone?

When I was co-minister of the congregation where they were members, Walter and Stella had been receiving Social Security as many years as I was old. Walter could not hear. Stella was knotted up with arthritis and could hardly move. When the phone rang, she thumped the floor with her cane. That got Walter's attention. He would pick up the phone and hold it to her ear while she talked. Suppose we had that kind of patience for one another as a congregation.

Love is not jealous. Hard to believe, but in nearly every congregation I have served or known, jealousy shows up. Over who is on the board and who is not. Over who are the pastor's close friends and who are not. Even at the seminary where I teach, nearly every semester I have students who are jealous over the fact that other students got higher grades.

Sometimes I think we should offer a course at the seminary in dealing with hurt feelings. Hurt feelings beget hurt feelings. Love begets love.

Love, Paul says, "does not insist on its own way." People who are full of the love of God do not take their pledges and stay home because they don't always get their way at church. People full of the love of God do not play tapes of past events over and over again, pointing out how the church should have done it their way.

Love "bears all things, believes all things, hopes all things, endures all things." We do not wither because someone is rude or insensitive, but accept others for who they are, and anticipate what they can become. And when things do not blossom as we expect–when so few show up for a meeting for which we have worked so hard, when someone lets us down, when we let someone else down–a loving person does not dwell on the failure, but looks to God and the future.

Sure, it's hard sometimes. The phone has been ringing, and people have been fanning the office door so fast you can't keep the pages settled on the desk long enough to read more than a sentence at a time, and someone comes in and says, "By the way, there's a crumb underneath the back corner of the refrigerator. Would you have it moved?" You may not feel kindly. But if you have experienced the love of which Paul speaks, then you have a better chance of responding not with hostility, but with the love that seeks the best for them, for you, for the congregation.

When I was a pastor in Nebraska, a young man came into our office. I was immediately suspicious because his clothes were wrinkled, even crusty. His shoes were old and cracked. His hair was shaggy and looked like soggy hay. He smelled. Because of the location of our building, we got such people all the time: a transient looking for money.

We had a program to deal with transients, and I was starting to put it into action. Then he told me his story.

A broken home. His mother died. His father wouldn't be responsible for him or his seven-year-old brother. The brother was taken from this young man because the young man was too young to be responsible for his brother. No place to call home, so he hit the road with a friend. They got as far west as Grand Island, Nebraska, when his friend left him sleeping in a park.

"Nobody cares," he said. "I'm looking for somebody who cares. I came here because I heard on the radio that Jesus cares."

What about it? Are you ready to be a conduit of the love of God for the men and women who walk into the door of your life?

Possibly a Porcupine Problem

Dale Andrews

I once came across an interesting clipping about the nocturnal habits of the spiny creature known to us as the porcupine. This clipping described some common sleeping patterns of the porcupine. During seasons of coldness, the porcupine will huddle in prone positions alongside each other trying to incubate within one another's body heat under the dire need to stay warm. But an incredibly interesting incident occurs during their evenings of rest. As the night grows colder, as they almost always do, the porcupine, instead of huddling even closer to one another to maintain some element of warmth, begin slowly to curl up within themselves. They curl up in the concerted effort to keep the cold out. As the porcupine slowly curl their bodies, their thorny quills begin to rise from their reposing position. As you can well imagine, this makes even the most casual snuggling a rather difficult task. The more the creatures curl up within themselves, the farther apart they become. And the farther they find themselves from one another, the colder they grow. The colder they grow, the more they curl. The more they curl, the colder they grow in a never-ending vicious circle of the ever futile attempt to stay warm. Definitely a perplexing porcupine problem!

In this letter to the Corinthians, Paul writes about some dissension within the church. Paul has heard from some people of the household of the matriarch named Chloe that there were divisions in their church. There was some quarreling. It seems that the people of Corinth were drawing lines between themselves. It seems that they would align themselves under the names of different leaders as if to represent some greater truth(s) among themselves, staking claim to some spiritual maturity or exclusive authority. Paul wants to know what has happened to cause such distancing from one another. If they are to be of the same mind and of the same judgment, then what kind of problem has caused them to lose their closeness? What kind of problem has grown? What kind of quills have risen between them? Well, could it not be described potentially as a porcupine kind of problem?

Paul begins to describe the scenario in the first chapter of his letter: One says, "I am of Paul!" Another asserts, "I am of Apollos!" While yet another proclaims, "I am of Cephas!" And of course, let us not overlook the one who responds, "I am of Christ!" Perhaps you can well imagine how this response resounds in a conversation about leadership, as if to suggest that their faction, unlike the others, was the only one that desired to be truly Christian. However, let us not be too critical of this last faction, for each group appears to function in kind. That is, by setting themselves under one name in the attempt to differentiate from others, they proclaim to possess some greater knowledge or awareness than their sisters or brothers. Does not such a divisive consciousness slowly destroy a community? The Corinthians had some pugnacious porcupine problems!

Now, proclaiming special insight does not necessarily have to divide. Paul is concerned about the peculiar and pervasive effects of such stands. Did the disagreements among the Corinthians need to disrupt their harmony? Must their quills remain standing on end? Should not some repose exist to allow them to enjoy not only what they have in common but also what they need from one another? Certainly, a poignant porcupine predicament!

Turning to "a still more excellent way" (1 Cor. 12:31), Paul tries to unite what the Corinthians have divided. Throughout this letter Paul has been concerned with the inward curl to self-centeredness and a party aggression highlighted by a severe state of arrogance, boasting, or spiritual elitism. Even the spiritual gifts themselves have become sources of authority for their divisions. Paul admonishes the Corinthians to enter a mature understanding of what it means to be members of a Christian community.

In "a still more excellent way," we must understand that our experiences of the Spirit, along with the spiritual gifts, must not become the stocks of disunity, alienation, or even privilege. Not only are individuals united with respect to the source of all spiritual gifts but they are also united in their purpose. As we can see from Paul's teaching, all persons do not receive the same gifts. Yet all gifts emanate from the one Spirit to whom we belong.

Indeed, in "a still more excellent way," we may understand that unity and diversity are cooperative interdependents. Spiritual gifts actually seem always to have "another" in mind and even serve the common good. It would appear that God has actually designed unity and diversity for the sake of a relational self, or the communal body itself, that there may be no discord. There is no room for rivalry or spiritual privilege. To behave so would detract from the very purpose of spiritual gifts and would split the community.

Paul does not endorse the divisions that the Corinthians have secured. He wishes to unite with Apollos. He seeks, if you will, to huddle alongside Apollos. Paul stresses the nature of church membership to be that of fellow workers. One may argue that he is referring to our being fellow workers with God, while another might assert that we are fellow workers with one another. Here, it might be especially useful to realize that the two are not necessarily mutually exclusive. Quite to the contrary, they seem to be mutually inclusive. Paul desires for those Corinthians holding to some Pauline virtue and those holding to some Apollonian virtue to sense and share some commonality, some unity, some sense of community. There is something special about a group of people sharing some sense of community. Moreover, there is something particularly special about sharing in a Christian community. When individuals bring and share their individuality in a communal effort, there is a oneness, a bonding, a body, "a still more excellent way."

There is a warmth that increases with closeness, but can only do so with willing participants. It is not a coincidental warmth, not a vain warmth, nor is it useless or without purpose. When we learn to huddle together, we find that it is a kind of warmth we need to withstand the coldness often encountered in this life. This warmth is something more than the warmth generated by one who stands alone. It is a warmth that is not attainable by the individual alone, nor is it attainable without the individual. We, as individuals, bring some kind of inner spirit that somehow grows in strength when it is shared and sought in community. Our contribution is necessary for the whole effect. When the biting and frigid winds of life's winters blow, there is something about the body of believers that cloaks the soul. We might feel the temptation to lean into the wind alone, or we can seek the sustaining, even strengthening, warmth of the collective body to get us and our sisters and brothers through the frosty night.

In the coldness of night our little friend the porcupine is just not able to stay warm. This is something that it is just not able to do by itself. The porcupine's ability to keep warm in cold times is directly proportional to how many other porcupines are sharing in the struggle to generate enough heat.

While each possesses some relative degree of warmth, none is sufficient alone. There is something dynamic about the warmth generated collectively. But each must bring its warmth, even along with its quills, to the effort. Surely we can begin to envision the potent promise of a porcupine partnership!

For "a still more excellent way," Paul stresses how special the faith community is. Now, one may possess the gift of prophetic powers and another the gift of knowledge, yet losing ourselves in theological quills, doctrinal spines, or spiritual privilege without some sense of oneness only results in factions of noncommunication and noncommunity, thereby distancing everyone not only from one another but also from our own effectiveness and greater understanding. Paul reminds the church of our oneness in Christ. Disagreeing is not necessarily a problem. The struggle to understand one another is not a problem either. It seems that Paul is most concerned with how the people of the church allow such unavoidable, even potentially useful, matters of life in the Christian experience to divide the community, to impede our care for the other. I believe Paul has some insight into the inflated danger of the porcupine problem. I believe Paul perceives the pretense of porcupine pomposity!

The community of believers is not only a gift where people enjoy fellowship and worship. It is also a crucial instrument in the development of each of us, the development of the kingdom of God and its mission. To divide the community is to lose the power of the community. We need each other! We need each other to talk with! We need each other to share with! We need each other to play with, to joke with, and to laugh with!—But we need each other for so much more—We need each other to cry with! We need each other to disagree with! We need each other to argue with, to learn from, to struggle with, and to seek understanding from! We need each other to experience the fullness of God! We need each other to experience what God holds for us, to experience love, even God's love! It is not that we are unable to experience God's love within ourselves. We must bring that love which God has for us, and the love we have for God, to our human relationships. When our relationships experience the nightfalls of a barren winter season,

I have got to believe, we have got to believe—even rely on and hope in—that there is something greater than ourselves that draws us together, and not just ourselves. As Paul insists, Christ is the foundation, and we—God's fellow workers!—a pack of porcupine partners prone to love…in a more excellent way!

Love

Eric D. Ash, Sr.

This is a public service announcement: There are only thirteen shopping days left till Saint Valentine's Day. Especially I want to remind the men of our congregation that now is the time to purchase chocolate candy hearts, or make reservations at a fancy restaurant, or buy one of those diamond tennis bracelets that Cindy Crawford tells us no woman's wardrobe is complete without. I don't want to boast, but I myself killed two birds with one stone by getting married on Valentine's Day. When I start seeing hearts and flowers in the stores, I think, "Hold on, this is supposed to mean something to me. I'm supposed to be remembering something important here."

The whole idea of how we celebrate Saint Valentine's Day is kind of ironic. In the early church, before it became legal to be a Christian in the fourth century C.E., there was a man, or perhaps actually two men, named Valentine. There are many legends about both of them that cannot be substantiated. However, it is undoubtedly true that both of them loved Christ and loved the church, and they were executed for their Christian faith. Somehow, maybe because the day of their deaths was close to a pagan festival celebrating human, carnal love, Valentine, or the Valentines, became associated with the idea of romantic love and the holiday we still celebrate today.

It's also kind of ironic that today's second reading, First Corinthians chapter 13, often called the love chapter, is the most requested reading at wedding services. Of the forty-eight marriage ceremonies I have performed, thirty of them here at Shiloh, we have read the love chapter at all but a handful of them. What's ironic is that in 1 Corinthians 13 Paul is only writing about romantic love, husband-and-wife love, in a secondary way. Paul's primary concern here is with the love of church members for one another.

The situation at the church in the City of Corinth was such that the congregation members disagreed with one another, slandered their leaders, and broke off into cliques. Hard for us to imagine, but true. Particularly it appears that the members at the First Church of Corinth were overly impressed with their own spiritual gifts. Some were said to work miracles. Others spoke in tongues. Those who possessed such gifts looked down on those who didn't and lorded it over them.

Paul wrote to the Corinthians to straighten out that sorry state of affairs. He said that it was okay to have spiritual gifts, but that spiritual gymnastics was not required to be a Christian. Everyone has their own calling, their own responsibilities, their own job to do; and God gives each of us the talents and skills necessary to do what he wants us to do. And no one person's calling is greater or lesser than another's. Paul places helpers and administrators in equal status with miracle workers and those who speak in tongues.

Yet even as equally wonderful as all the spiritual gifts are, there is, Saint Paul says, one gift that outshines all the others. There is something much more important than spiritual gymnastics and something that every Christian is called to do. And that something is love.

Now as we said earlier, Paul primarily was addressing here the love of Christians for one another. But that certainly does include, in an important, albeit secondary, way, the love found in families and especially the love between a man and a woman. Especially it is important today, as the institution of marriage and the family seem to be crumbling before our eyes, for the church to address, "What is love?"

Love as Saint Paul used, and the church uses, the word, needs to be defined. Love is not the warm, fuzzy feeling you get when you are around someone you like to be with, someone who gives you the momentary illusion that all is right with the world. That's infatuation, not love. Love is not an emotion, contrary to popular belief. Love is also not the craving we have for physical intimacy. That's lust, not love. And we've all seen the trouble that unchecked lust can cause. And love is not dependency. Some people become completely dependent on another person to provide for their every need. Other people seem to enjoy waiting on others hand and foot and get some kind of twisted pleasure out of being taken advantage of and abused. That's not love; that's psychological pathology.

I think Christian author and professional psychiatrist M. Scott Peck came pretty close to adequately defining love in the Christian context in his best-selling book a few years back called *The Road Less Traveled*. Dr. Peck begins the book by pointing out that, as we all know, life is hard and full of problems. And most of us keep right on wallowing in our miseries, making the same mistakes over and over again, stuck in the same old ruts because we don't have the will, the courage, and especially the self-discipline to confront our problems and solve them.

But when we do exercise the discipline to confront our problems, then we grow spiritually. And that's how Peck defines love, as the will, the motivation, the act of extending oneself for the purpose of our own or another's spiritual growth. In that way then, love can be seen as a commitment we choose to make. It can be seen as a sacrifice we choose to make as we delay our gratifications, and bear burdens, and run the risk of pain in the present for the sake of spiritual growth in the future. And most of all, love is hard work. It requires discipline, or what is often called today "tough love."

This is love Christ modeled for us. He did not relax the law one iota; he did not ignore the wrong we had done; and he did not promise us that life would be a rose garden. Instead he bore the burden of our sins, withstood the agony of the cross, and taught us how to be better people, all so that we could be reborn of water and the Spirit, and live and reign with him in eternity, despite our unworthiness.

When people ask me what makes a marriage last or what makes a family successful, my usual answer is "commitment," the commitment only made possible by pure Christian love. If two marriage partners or two family members are truly committed to each other, then they can forgive each other their faults through all the ups and downs, and joys and sorrows that life brings. And then they can believe all things, hope all things, and endure all things just as Saint Paul said.

Through the eyes of the world the obligations of marriage partners and family members to one another might seem overwhelming and inescapable. Only in faith can we see those obligations as not only tolerable but also holy and joyous. It's true that love is hard work, but love is also the greatest joy, the greatest gift God has given us as well.

Recent sociological and psychological studies have shown that there is a single characteristic of families that seems to be correlated to producing healthy family relationships, high-achieving children, and so on. And that one characteristic that these successful families share is that they eat meals together regularly. It's sad but true that in today's busy world many families literally never share a meal together. It seems to me that somehow family mealtime is a primary place where love gets shared.

In a similar way, the holy communion is the family meal of the church. Here Christ shares his love with us in word and liturgy, in bread and wine, in body and blood. And we who take part in this Christian family meal not only know that we are loved eternally, but are strengthened to get out there when the church service is over and love our families, love our husbands or wives if we have them, and love all humanity in general and in particular with the love we have first received. That is the divine love Christ has for us.

Amen.

The Excellent Way

Deborah Avery

I have to tell you that I am very excited by the opportunity to worship with you this evening, but because I am a seminary student and a mother of two children, with my homework piling up around my ears, and housework...Well, I'd rather not talk about housework. I wasn't sure how I could possibly pull together a worship service and a sermon and still manage to get a few hours of sleep! Yet somehow, God provided me with sufficient energy and time, and here we are!

When I selected this text, I soon became aware that I set before myself a rather awesome task. As I began to prepare this meditation, I asked myself, How in the world can I say anything new about these verses of scripture that are so well known? They are quoted in songs and used in wedding homilies. The last phrase in verse 13 has become a kind of slogan used in a wide variety of situations: "And the greatest of these is love." I even remember a song from my childhood years: "Have faith, hope, and charity, that's the way to live successfully. How do I know? The Bible tells me so." With all that history that has gone before me, I wondered what new insights I could possibly find.

After grappling with these questions for quite a while, I decided to let Paul speak for himself, for it is in the voice of the apostle that we can hear his gospel message of love and reconciliation as it was addressed to a fragmented Christian community in the city of Corinth.

The city of Corinth had a strong tradition of being in a strategic location. It was a port city—a major stopping place for ships on the sea route between Rome and Ephesus. And it was on the wild route between Sparta and Athens. The city was both a political capital and a commercial capital for the surrounding region. It was a bustling, enterprising place with opportunities for anyone who cared to make an effort. The citizens were active in business and were doing a lot of social "ladder climbing." It was definitely an every-man-for-himself environment, a dog-eat-dog world in which the savvy businessman or astute society host or hostess could earn much power and prestige. In that way, Corinth is not unlike our own strategic position here in Montgomery County. As I listened to election returns, it seemed that Montgomery City was the crucial political center for so many offices. The governor's reelection was attributed to his strong support in Montgomery County. While Gaithersburg may not be the political capital that Washington is, we are located in that vital commercial and industrial "technology corridor," and many people come here to work, shop, seek medical care, and entertain themselves.

When we look closely at the Corinthians, we find a broken community. Their ladder-climbing, hierarchical thinking has caused divisions among them—divisions between the haves and the have-nots, disagreements over wisdom and the true teachings. Yet in the opening words of First Corinthians, Paul commends them and offers thanks, reminding them of the many gifts they have been given through Christ. He recognizes in them a great and wonderful potential to serve God in amazing ways. But somehow the Corinthians still got it all wrong, and Paul is quick to point it out. They, too, recognize their gifts, but use them to raise their status. While they acknowledge Christ's grace in their lives, they act as though that somehow removes all responsibility from them. So, when we see them through Paul's eyes, we see their drunken behavior at the eucharistic gatherings. We find immoral sexual behavior. We find individuals using their gifts to elevate their own personal status. The Corinthians behave as though they are completely unaware of the connection they have to one another through Christ and the responsibility that comes with the life in Christ Jesus.

So when we hear this part of the letter, we are hearing Paul offer the Corinthians the antidote to the disease of brokenness. That antidote is love–the self-emptying love of Christ–the excellent way. All the many gifts the Corinthians have received are worthless unless they are put to use with the same love as shown by Jesus Christ, whose ultimate act was to give of himself for others.

This is the love about which Paul speaks. In this letter to the Corinthians, Paul is not seeking to condemn them for their sinful behavior. He is not engaged in the finger-pointing of a self-righteous person. He wants to show them how to join together as the body of Christ.

Paul is speaking to us too. For we are not very much different from the Corinthians. Their brokenness is our brokenness; their sins are our own. Where they failed, we too fail. How many ways are we Christians fragmented? How many of us have experienced a broken relationship or an unkind act? How many times have we ourselves acted self-righteously? Yes, we can learn from Paul too. We, too, need to experience the healing, unifying Spirit of love that comes from Christ Jesus. We, too, need to use our special gifts with that loving Spirit.

There has never been any question that we are a gifted community. Each one of us has something to offer. These gifts have been given to us by God through the power of the Holy Spirit. Some of us have the gift of music, others of preaching or public speaking. Some of us serve on council with the gift of administration. Some of us are teachers, some are helpers, and still others have the gift of doing kind acts. But it isn't enough just to have the gift. For if we use our gift of music without love in our hearts, we might as well be banging on pots and pans. If we teach impatiently, or give only when we're sure to receive something in return, our gift is useless. When we use our gifts as a way of building up our own lives, it is as if we have no gift at all.

When we follow the excellent way–the way of love–our gifts will be used in a Christlike manner. The excellent way to use our gift will not tear us down, but will strengthen and build us up. When we use our gifts through the power of Christ's love, we will not be divided, for that love will bind us together. The love of Christ is a unifying force. We must let love be the constant. Love will be the glue that binds us together. For when everything else passes away, when there is nothing else left, the love of Christ will endure forever.

Amen.

The Rule of Love

Daniel V. Biles, III

First Corinthians 13—we hear it at weddings, read it in poetry books, find it on greeting cards. Homiletics professors say it needs no sermon to explain it; just read the text and proceed with the service. The beauty and simplicity of its language make it a sentimental favorite, a natural choice for those moments when we look for a way to express our thoughts or feelings, no matter how temporary they may be. It sounds so nice, so romantic, so beautiful. That's why it's such a popular passage of scripture. Paul did not feel romantic when he wrote it. He intended his "Love Hymn" as a hard-driving attack on an unchristian lifestyle. In it he powerfully asserted what should be the basis for Christian life with others. To a church torn by disputes over who was the most "spiritual," to a congregation split by factions arguing over the authentically Christian way of doing things, Paul put forward "the more excellent way" of self-giving love.

Time and usage have blunted Paul's words and reduced his proposed norm for the Christian lifestyle to the sort of wishy-washy, sugary-sweet sentiment popular on Valentine's Day. Perhaps we need to hear Paul's message in a fresh way, in words he might have used had he been writing to our church today:

Now, you are the body of Christ and individually members of it. God has appointed in the church many people with different tasks and gifts to do his work. He has called out first pastors, those men and women whose specific job is to preach and teach the Word of God first spoken by the apostles as it speaks to us today. But God also speaks through other people, men and women of all backgrounds who may at any given moment have a special insight into God's will for God's church. There are teachers, those given the special responsibility and honor of passing on to the next generation the wisdom of the Bible and the Christian tradition gathered over the centuries. There are helpers, administrators, leaders, and those with special gifts and abilities given by God. Not everyone has the same gift or ability, nor should they. But everyone, from the great to the least, the poorest to the richest, the eldest to the youngest, has a special contribution to make and a task to do. Yet to all of you is given a gift that should shape and direct your thoughts, words, and actions. It has been called the gift of love, and it is still the most excellent basis for living of all.

God made you and destined you to love and be loved. If you do not know this as true for your own life, all is sheer waste and vanity, even if you should accomplish all that which humans call successful, glorious, and honorable. You may have the virtue of a saint and enjoy the respect of all, but without love that is able to care for others, your life is empty and dead. You may fulfill your human potential, succeed at the game of self-realization, but without self-giving love that risks and shares commitments to others, you have lost everything and realized nothing. You may create for yourself a comfortable standard of living, abound in material wealth; yet so long as one person is downtrodden, outcast, exploited, denied the opportunity to have what you have, then you are just as poor as he and just as much in need of liberation. You may create for yourselves the most powerful economic, military, and political nation on earth, yet without love that expresses itself in justice and the quest of peace, you have gained nothing of lasting importance. If in your creativity and power you should find a way to conquer all, explore the universe, and master creation, yet have not learned through love how to live with creation and each other, your accomplishments are small indeed. And if you should gain all knowledge, and by your technology become as a god, doing all things, even creating human life itself, yet have not learned through love what it means to be a human being and are without morality, all is vain. All you have and are and do, if it is not shaped by the same self-giving, suffering love God has shown you in Jesus Christ, is vain indeed.

Love—such as that which comes from God—occurs this way. Love does not exploit others but shows concern for the real needs of the other person. Love does not seek personal revenge, but seeks to establish and maintain fellowship even in the face of hurt and anger. Love does not shirk the truth, but speaks the truth honestly and with caring, without pretension, criticism, judgment, or flattery. Love does not glory in division and conflict, but presses onward in hope for reconciliation and a new beginning. Love does not withdraw in lonely, cynical isolation, but even at the risk of being vulnerable seeks commitment, caring, and a shared life with others. Love is not a casual affair, a fleeting emotion, an easy-come, easy-go matter, but expresses itself in faithfulness and dependability through time. This is how love occurs. This is how God works among us.

As for the things that people regard as important and necessary in life, all these things shall have their time and place and in due time pass away. Fads and fancies will come and go, whims and wishes will catch our attention for a moment and soon fade. Empires and nations will rise and fall. Great issues and crises will come, leave their marks, and then disappear. Great deeds will be done and soon forgotten. Careers will flourish and fade; children will grow up and leave home; what was once so necessary and critical to life will in time seem immaterial and of small consequence. As for our way of life, it will change. All these things will have their day, their hour, their moment of significance, but all shall change and pass away.

But what will never cease to be new and of value and importance is love, the gift of sharing life with others. It is love, a life of faithfulness and mutual self-giving with others, that is the one thing whose value lasts though times and fashions change. It is to this end–to love–that you were created, and this is the future for which God has destined you. He has sealed this in the death and resurrection of Jesus. Because Jesus lives, free from the power of death to destroy, his love shall rule in our lives. What we seek and strive for today–faithfulness from others, caring, nurturing families, fulfilling marriages, peace on earth, healthy communities–all this will find its fulfillment as it is joined together in the coming rule of love that the risen Lord Jesus will bring. For now we only have hints and foretastes of what is to come, of the future Jesus prepares and the love that will rule in it. The care and nurture of a mother for her child; the steadfast love of a husband and wife that stands the test of time; fragile, hidden moments of forgiveness and reconciliation; moments of peace amid the gathering storms of war; the helping hand reaching out to another in need; God's own hand reaching out to ours in forms of bread and wine: These and more are but a hint of what is to come. Most of all, we have seen a glimpse, however dim, in the story of the God who suffers in love for others in the man Jesus of Nazareth. His love shall overrule our divisions and succeed where we have failed. His love, which identifies with the ungodly, the outcast, the broken and rejected of the world, will encompass our lives and the lives of all people and join them in one fellowship.

And so there are three things that every person in life needs: someone or something to trust in completely (this we call God), a future to dream and hope for, and love to receive and give with others. Without these, no person can live. But what is needed most of all is love. Through love we realize what it means to be human. Through love we come to know God, who has shown us love as he became human in Jesus Christ. And it is his love that shall rule.

To this I can only add: May his love rule in your lives this day and every day.

Amen.

This Thing Called Love

Dale S. Bringman

Love! Perhaps no word is used or misused more frequently. *Love* is a catch-all word. To paraphrase Elizabeth Barrett Browning: How do we love? Let us count the ways. We love football and family, peach pie and puppies, houses and cars, money and mates, friends and finances, and yes, we love God. Each is an emotion, but not all are the same. If a husband loves his wife and his car in the same way, he may be driving a spiffy Ferrari, but when he gets home, his wife will be gone.

Some languages are more precise, distinguishing between the love for an object, the affection for a friend, and the sensual erotic love between a man and a woman. In the writings of Saint Paul, the apostle always uses the special word *agape* when he writes about love. *Agape* is the love of God given freely in Jesus Christ. It holds nothing back and demands nothing in return. It is poured out even to the lowliest and the least deserving. It is the love exemplified in Paul's salutary observation that "while we were still sinners Christ died for us" (Rom. 5:8).

This love of God is different. "See what manner of love the Father has given us," we read in the first letter of John (1 Jn. 3:1, author's translation). The phrase "See what manner," sometimes simply translated as "See," is an idiom one might find familiar:

> See what manner of ship this is. It was different from all the others!

God's love, *agape*, is like that: delightfully different, unearthly, and wonderful. Significantly, when Saint Paul exhorts us to love, he uses this same word. We are to love the way God loves, but none of us can love like that on his or her own. What the apostle is telling us is that we must let the love of God fill us so completely that this love of God in us spills over to others. This *agape* isn't our love at all. We are simply channels. It is God's love moving in and through us. This love is not the superlative degree of *like* as if we liked someone or something more and more until we came to love that person or thing.

That may describe one kind of love, perhaps the love for skiing or for a person, but that isn't what Paul is describing. *Agape* is the love of God in us that enables us to love people we don't even like. It makes it possible for us to do things we don't want to do. It is the love God bestows upon us, the love that trudged ignominiously to the cross and was raised from the dead. It is the love that fills us when we, with Paul, "know whom we have believed," experiencing that Jesus Christ is our Savior and Lord and accepting God's acceptance of us. It is no longer we who love, but Christ who lives and loves in us. This *agape* is the theme Paul details in his first letter to the Corinthians, in which he claims that this love *excels, expresses, and endures.*

Love excels beyond all modes of speaking. Often we yearn to speak wiser and better. We hear something profound and wish we had said that. We look back on conversations and think of things we might have said. Yet this love of God is greater than the most profound elocution or the most insightful utterance. *Agape* surpasses the polished eloquence of people and the sonorous voices of angels. Noisy gongs and clanging cymbals are used by some religious people to awaken their gods so that the gods will hear their prayers. These, however, are woefully ineffective and useless, but no more so than is eloquent speech compared with love.

How great it would be, too, if we could know the future and could tell with certainty what will happen and could prepare for it. Perhaps even more tremendous would be the ability to unravel the mysteries of the solar system or the genetic code, to have all knowledge about all things. Our minds can scarcely grasp what Paul is saying when he writes that love surpasses even that.

Love is a cherished gift. It enables us to hang on when all else fails. Sacrifice, too, is a prime virtue, as one unceasingly goes the second mile, and may even involve the giving of one's life like that of a martyr burned at a stake. Yet love is greater even than us. It is the "love divine, all loves excelling." *Agape* excels beyond all others.

Love expresses itself in tangible ways. It is not simply some lofty ideal without relationship to daily life. It is patient in an impatient world wherein the turning of a stop light to green evokes the blowing of horns, the tardiness of a hoped-for response brings violence and death, and the slowness of a weaker nation to comply triggers sanctions and air strikes. Love waits it out and is kind. It doesn't lord itself over others and insist that only its way is right.

On a person-to-person level *agape* doesn't rejoice in wrongdoing. How different that is from our culture, which gloats over the failures of others. Become a candidate for public office, and someone is certain to dig up salacious tidbits from some 25-year-old experience. After all, rejoicing in the truth doesn't sell newspapers or increase TV ratings. How different this is from love that bears all things, ever aware that our heaviest burdens can't begin to compare with the weight of a cross on the back of one who stumbled his way to Golgotha for us. Love believes the best in another person, never the worst. It ties a knot of hope on the rope of life and hangs on to the very end. Love expresses itself gloriously in every relationship in life.

Love endures. When experiences are good, we like them to last. That trip to the mountains or that cruise on the Caribbean seems to end all too soon. The longer we live, the more we realize how few things really last. Friends move. Relatives die. In the words of the Greek philosopher Heraclitus, everything is in a state of flux. Life is like standing in a stream. We look down at the water only to see it flowing away to be replaced by other water. Saint Paul echoes this truth, writing that prophecies, tongues, and knowledge pass away. We know only in part. In our fast-paced world we constantly see knowledge being replaced by newer inventions and understandings. We may think we see something clearly only to discover that our knowledge is like looking into a cloudy mirror where we see only partial and distorted images. Everything changes and passes away. Ross Parker, who wrote, "There will always be an England," had a patriotism that was better than his theology. Ogden Nash put it succinctly: "The great God Ra / whose shrine once covered acres. Is filler now / for crossword puzzle-makers." "Change and decay in all around I see." "Yet amid all the changes in life, love is constant. God is love and as he was in the beginning, is now and ever shall be."

Love doesn't end. It spills over from this life to the next. There we shall know and be fully known. The simple tombstone epitaph is true: "You think I'm forgot, but I'm not." In God's good time and way, God will call us to God'self, and we shall hear the invitation: "Come you that are blessed of my Father, inherit the kingdom prepared for you from the foundation of the world" (Mt. 25:34). "Faith, hope and love abide, these three, but the greatest of these is love" (1 Cor. 13:13).

The story of Pygmalion has been retold in many forms, one being the Broadway musical *My Fair Lady*. The original story in Greek mythology portrays Pygmalion as a sculptor who despised women. He hated them vehemently, and so to show how inferior women were, Pygmalion decided to carve a statue of an exquisite woman. His statue, by comparison, would show the deficiencies of women. Pygmalion sculpted long and devotedly. He chiseled and polished, and with his skillful hands created a strikingly beautiful, perfect statue of a woman. Her face, her hair, and her perfectly proportioned shape were without parallel. Then a strange thing happened. Pygmalion fell in love with the statue he had made. He would kiss those cold stone lips. He would caress the hands and face. He would take the statue in his arms and embrace it passionately. He would dress it in fine clothes and buy gifts for the statue. Pygmalion was hopelessly in love with a lifeless thing. In Greek mythology, of course, anything can happen. The Feast Day of Venus was being celebrated on the island of Cyprus. Pygmalion went there and asked Venus for a living woman as lovely as the statue he had carved. When Pygmalion returned, he, in his wonted way, embraced the statue he loved and pressed his warm lips against those rigid unresponsive ones. Suddenly, he felt warm arms clutching him, and he felt those cold lips becoming soft and warm and luscious. He touched the wrists and felt blood pulsing through the body. He saw a smile in the eyes and a blush on the face. The statue he had made and loved had become alive. This impossibly beautiful woman was responding to his love.

God has created all of us, and God loves us with a steadfast love that never ends or dies. Often we must seem to God like lifeless statues, cold and unresponsive. Yet God's love will not let us go. God's love is from everlasting to everlasting. Unceasingly God loves us, so much so that God sent God's only son that whoever believes in Him may have everlasting life. By God's grace we are filled with God's *agape,* God's love, which *excels, expresses, and endures.* Then, and only then, do we know what is this thing called love.

The Temporal and the Eternal[2]

Emil Brunner

> Love never faileth: but whether there be prophecies, they shall be done away: whether there be tongues, they shall cease; whether there be knowledge, it shall be done away. For we know in part, and we prophesy in part: but when that which is perfect is come, that which is in part shall be done away. When I was a child, I spake as a child, I felt as a child, I thought as a child: now that I am become a man, I have put away childish things. For now we see in a mirror, darkly; but then face to face: now I know in part; but then I shall know even as also I have been known. But now abideth faith, hope, love, these three; and the greatest of these is love. (1 Cor. 13:8–13, author's translation)

In these latter years we have been made to experience in a particularly alarming manner how all things human are subject to the law of *change and decay.* Those of us who are older still remember how very different was the feeling of life in our younger days. We then considered so many things to be firmly and unshakably founded, which have subsequently been dashed to pieces in the onward rush of the time stream. How fantastically has the map of Europe been changed; powerful empires have arisen and again vanished; the whole centre of gravity of the political world has completely shifted within the space of a few decades. The solid gains of civilization, such as the security of life and property and personal freedom, which we held to be permanent attainments, have to a large extent disappeared, and, on the other hand, phenomena of earlier periods, such as tyranny, barbarism, slavery, and the persecution of Christians, which we had thought to have been permanently abolished, have again become a reality. The whole structure of life to its very centre seems convulsed, insecure, and questioned.

Is there anything at all which has solidity? Is there anything for which the world of the poet is not valid when he says that everything which stands is only fit for destruction? Of course there is something exciting and fascinating about the idea that, as people say, things are in a state of flux. But life itself grows monstrous, indeed meaningless, if all is in a state of unending flux and imminent dissolution, just as what lends terror to an earthquake is precisely the fact that everything collapses, even the most solid thing–the earth itself. Of course we feel very comforted as we sing somewhat unreflectingly with Paul Gerhardt, "All passes away," but do we at the same time realize what it would mean if it were really true that all passes away? It would imply nothing less than that life as a whole is purposeless. And it is just that which is the feeling to which many today have succumbed and by which we are all more or less infected: Everything is in a state of dissolution, nothing is unshakable, hence nothing abides; there is nothing which emerges permanently from the flux, there is no irremovable goal, no unchanging direction, no eternal meaning behind the revolutions of time. If that is indeed the case, then life is truly a madhouse, full of sound and fury, signifying nothing.

The Word of Scripture which we have just read to some extent confirms this general impression. In this chapter too, which is so often misunderstood and misapplied in a sentimental sense, the apostle Paul shows himself to be a great realist who sees things exactly as they are. Yes, he declares that transiency is truly the characteristic mark of our life here below. Even the greatest values which the Christian community has experienced and highly prizes he sees to be caught up in the unending flux of time. The word of the prophet, which in the main was the very life of primitive Christian worship, passes away–that, for us, so mysterious seizure by the divine spirit which he describes as speaking with tongues, also passes away; the recognition of ultimate divine truths to which the apostle Paul in particular had turned his mind and so largely contributed, again passes away. We might go on: not only all that we call culture and civilization, but also the Church itself, the sacraments and preaching–all that, too, passes away. For all this is integrally bound up with our earthly state, with temporality and imperfection—or, as we say today, with relativity. Even our apprehension of the divine revelation—this is what Paul means by knowledge—forms no exception. For, so reasons the apostle, what we now recognize as truth is something merely partial, not the rounded whole. Because and in so far as it is partial, it belongs to the sphere of the temporal and changing. It would have been good if the Church had taken more seriously this lesson of its greatest human teacher; it would then have been less easily a victim of the temptation to establish this or that formulation of its insight as an eternally valid, irrevocable dogma. For again and again it has been seen that even those supposed timelessly valid dogmas contained an element of the purely human and so of the changing. And it would be all to the good if precisely we theologians recalled more often this insight—that all knowledge is partial. Then we would be less inclined to present our theses in an absolute and systematic manner and to accuse each other of heresy.

Please do not forget, Paul here suggests, that so long as you live on earth and are clothed in this earthly body, you go about, so to speak, in child's shoes. Maturity, true maturity of fulfillment, does not exist here. Even the greatest teachers err; there remains something unsatisfying and premature even in them and their thought. Even they must be corrected, even their message may not be taken without more ado as the last word of wisdom. This is felt above all by those who most zealously and passionately wrestle to attain truth. One of the most striking things about so doughty a Biblical exegete as Martin Luther—a feature which constantly reconciles us to much with which we are inclined to disagree in his writings—is that he emphasizes again and again that he is only a beginner and has not got beyond the rudiments of Scriptural interpretation, that every day he must learn afresh in a discipline which has no end. In fact, it is precisely one of the notes of true greatness that a man should feel that he is only groping with the beginnings of insight and wisdom, always as it were only in the first stages, not only as regards knowledge but also in regard to the character of Christian living generally.

And our test suggests to us a second image on which to ponder. All our knowledge is only a seeing through a glass darkly. As long as we see merely the reflection of a human being in a mirror, we do not make real contact with him; we do not see him face-to-face. And moreover what we thus see and recognize is in the last resort unsatisfying and incomplete. There clings to all that we can affirm about God, Jesus Christ, creation and redemption, a certain characteristic contradictoriness. Such doctrines are not lucid and self-evident like a theorem in Euclid; they are to be described rather as a mystery—a mystery which must always remain impenetrable to us. If we teach and speak as though we were dealing with self-evident mathematical truth, we are teaching falsely; then the most essential thing is lacking, viz., the consciousness of mystery and impenetrability. Just for that reason our insights must be partial and always subject to correction. Unsolved and insoluble questions there must always be. We never reach the end; we are back always only at the beginning.

Is there then nothing which has unshakable solidity, of which we might say: That will abide, that is eternal? The apostle Paul is certainly a realist, but he is no relativist. He does not allow us to be engulfed in eddies of incertitude. We catch the reverberation of his words in another passage: *"For I am certain"* (Rom. 8:38–39). In truth, he preaches the gospel not as something uncertain, merely relative and transient. He knows of course that we carry this treasure in earthen vessels, that the treasure itself is embedded in human words and ideas and that the latter are temporal and passing because relative and incomplete. But the revelation is of God and therefore eternal. In what does this eternal and ultimately valid element consist? Do we somehow possess it otherwise than in the mode of merely human insights? Is there something in the actuality of Christian living of which we may and must say: there is the heart of the matter, the truly divine, which therefore abides unconditionally and absolutely?

To this our text gives answer, unlike many fine-spun theologies: yes, indeed, there is such an element, and it is love. But at this point we must beware lest we make a mistake which would confuse us about this very issue. Natural human love universally known is not here in question. The love of a mother, the love of husband and wife, the love of friends, the love of country—all are beautiful, good, and necessary things, but they are not here in question. For all that is something natural, beautiful, of course, but still merely human. This Biblical message points to something which is not natural, but supernatural, something which is not human but wholly other, wholly divine.

What then has God disclosed to us in Jesus Christ? The fact that God is love. I wish I had the mastery of words that I might bring home to you the enormous significance of this affirmation, which in our Sunday school days we sang about in a hymn I am tempted to describe as unfortunately sentimental: "God is love." It is the most amazing, incomprehensible pronouncement that was ever made in human language. Never previously had a philosopher or a treatise on religion formulated just this: God is love. If Plato or Aristotle had heard such a statement, they would have shaken their heads and replied: "Man, you are mad, you do not know what you are talking about." How can God be love, indeed how can God experience love at all, since He has all and needs nothing and is wholly self-sufficient? What we are accustomed to call love is always a need for completion, a striving after something which one feels the lack of.

It is only within the sphere of biblical revelation that love is described in exactly the opposite way. There we hear about a love which does not desire anything but simply bestows itself—a love which does not spring from any need or lack but has its source in overflowing richness and plenitude of life. "God loves you" does not imply "God needs you or longs for you," but that He gives and sacrifices Himself for your sake. Because of that the cross of Jesus Christ is the revelation of divine love, of the love which God not merely has but which is His very life. This love, true love, self-bestowing love, as opposed to claimful love, love which flows from inexhaustible wealth rather than from want—just that is the being of God. And if we propose to speak of God, then we must speak of Him in terms of such love.

But I have not yet expressed the matter rightly. We only view it from the right angle when we bring into play the second person singular. God loves *you*. He wills to bestow Himself upon *you*. He wills to have fellowship with you, with you in whom

He can find nothing lovely, simply because He wills to impart to you what is worthy of love—Himself. Consider well, this message comes to you not from some human source, from some religion or philosophy. It is addressed to you solely and exclusively in the glad tidings of Jesus Christ. God loves you, sinful man. God loves you and comes to seek you, as the shepherd seeks his lost sheep, the woman her lost coin, to find which she upsets the whole house. Yes, God has upset the whole universe in order to find you, His lost coin. He has come to us in the form of man, in the form of a crucified Saviour, so that no one can say: It is not me He is looking for, He does not want to know me. It is just you He seeks, you who feel so unworthy of being loved by Him. Just that is the meaning of the Gospel.

Thus God addresses you now in these words of mine and otherwise in the whole Bible. What answer will you make to Him? What answer would God like to have from you? What does He expect? He would like, He expects, that you quite simply believe what He says, that you accept it and rejoice because He loves you. That is what the New Testament means by faith. This utter simplicity of heart which causes you to accept the proffered love of God, to overcome your doubt that it might not be so, might not be God who is so speaking, and to take His outstretched hand.

And what happens now when you really do this, when with all your heart you grasp the love of God offered to you in Jesus Christ? Look, you do not then merely acquire the love of God, but it is rather that the love of God then penetrates your being with the result that a new life begins in you. Then you become a being who loves, then there grows in your garden something which is not of this world and its glory, which passeth away, but a plant of divine heavenly and eternal origin—nothing other than this very love which flows from the heart of God Himself. This love, our text assures us, cannot pass away because it is eternal in its very essence. It is the thing with which all life is concerned and for the achievement of which we and the whole world have been created. It constitutes our eternal end; it is eternal life. It alone remains when all else passes away, because it has its source wholly in the being of God, in eternity.

What then are we to say about the relationship of faith and love? Simply this: faith is the opening of the human heart to the penetration of divine love. It is the human hand which grips the proffered love of God. Faith is so important because it is the power by which we appropriate that love. And yet faith itself is not eternal but transient. For at the last it must so be that we need no longer believe because we shall live utterly in the animating presence of the love of God. But in the present order faith must always utter its "in spite of": in spite of the fact that I am a sinner, God loves me. In spite of the fact that the world is so loveless, God the Creator and Lord of the world is love. In spite of the fact that Jesus Christ is the Crucified, He is the Son of God who took upon Him our flesh, who for our sakes became man, the incarnate love of God. In spite of the fact that I shall die, there is in me, inwoven into the roots of my being, the eternal love of God, the very life of eternity triumphant over death. This "in spite of" is nothing else but an expression of that obscurity which causes us to see only through a glass darkly. But there will come a time when the "in spite of" vanishes away. There will come a time when the opposition between sinful humanity and the divine is overcome and ceases to be. Then we shall no longer be confined to this earthly imperfect mode of the knowledge of God. Such knowledge will then be transcended by something far higher, namely, by the vision face-to-face. And therein lies the perfect and unchanging, towards which by faith our sure and certain hope is directed.

Faith knows that such is the eternal end. But so long as we must live by faith we have not yet attained it. Hence, the end is always something other than what we now enjoy. We cherish the goal in the form of *hope,* a securely based, firm and steadfast hope, but nevertheless only hope. But when the end is reached and fulfillment comes, then we shall experience it no longer as hope but as plenitude of life and presence. For that reason, then, hope too, like faith, will vanish away. One thing will then remain unchanged: the love of God which we now apprehend in our hearts by faith. That does not pass away, nor does it need to be transformed. It is the unchanging and eternal, the being of God Himself, eternal life.

Now remain faith, hope and love, these three. Faith, the unsealing of the heart, the hand outstretched to make our own the love of God; hope, which assures us of future fulfillment by the perfecting of our fellowship with God; and love. Faith looks back to what God has done and imparted. It sees how God cancels our past sins and forgives us in the name of Jesus Christ. Faith appropriates that past event in which God founds our life anew as the life of children of God who through the covenant of Jesus Christ have been adopted out of the status of aliens into that of sons of God.

By faith we live today in the power of what God has once done. And on the other hand hope points to the future of which we are already heirs, but which we do not inherit so long as we remain in this earthly fleshly life. By hope we hold fast to our future consummation as a good which really belongs to us through the work of Jesus Christ. As faith is concerned with the past and hope with the future, so love gives us fullness of life in the present. For the love of God is shed abroad in our hearts, and we have appropriated the gift by faith. But this divine love is effectively present with us and makes us truly alive in the present. For where love is, there arises *plenitude of being and reality in the present moment;* where love is not, one is not truly alive to the urgencies of the present, but lives in regret and grief for the past, or in anxiety about the future. Solely through the power of love can we be creatively alive in communion with our fellow men, really devoted to them and sensitive to their needs, so that they note of us: such a one is truly attentive to me, his heart is not elsewhere. But love is above all things the eternal "now"–that which fills eternity with its radiance and joy, and in the power of which God will be fully present to us and we to Him.

And thus of these three theological virtues, which are so closely interwoven, love is the greatest. Faith is not God Himself. God does not believe. And hope is not God, for God does not hope. But God is love, for God Himself loves and is love in its changeless living reality. Because God is greater than all things, therefore love is greater than any other virtue, greater even than faith and hope.

Let not your hearts be troubled about the transiency of all earthly things: only be steadfast, through faith and hope in the love of God. That is the crucial issue. Whoever can thus stand fast, can do the best of which any human being is capable. And whoever cannot do that, falls short of the best, however able, however great a genius he may be in other respects. The changeless and abiding is love, is God. All else passes away: that alone remains. All else is only reflected light, reflected in the painted dome of earthly life. But love is the white radiance of eternity. Therefore let us live in the strength of love, which God has bestowed upon us in our Lord Jesus Christ.

To Have and to Hold
Gerald Christianson

We, your families and friends, are grateful that you have brought us together for this wedding—grateful because we can renew old memories, express gratitude long overdue, share new experiences, and, most important, discover new relationships. In appreciation, we will shower you with gifts. My happy responsibility is to offer you, on behalf of the entire company, the first and most significant.

It is a gift, says Paul, the author of that beautiful letter to the Corinthians, that is beyond hope and even faith. It is, says the psalmist, steadfast and endures forever. It is, of course, the gift of love. My challenge is how to describe it.

The gift I received the day you asked me to preside at your wedding was the opportunity to explore the Hebrew Bible for a model of a loving relationship. I think we find a most profound and provocative one right here in this company. You are two individuals who have come together, but you also represent two families, two cultures, and two religions. We have never been on the best of terms, we Jews and Christians. We got off to a rocky start, and our infamous love affair has never significantly improved, especially not during the last century when we went to the brink of the unthinkable.

We have tarnished the love we were given as our joint heritage. We have tempered it with the fires of misunderstanding, petty pride, and downright prejudice. Yet we are still together. If we can't seem to live with each other, we most certainly can't live without each other.

I think God wants it this way. He wants to show the world through us—through our failings, our quarrels, and conflicts—not only that we are very human but that despite all this he is faithful to us; that only his love can empower our love; that our love will be unfulfilled unless and until it comes from him. I think he wants the world to learn from our stormy marriage what kind of God he is.

Consider this God who keeps us together. What characteristic comes to mind when you think of Him? Big, awesome, distant, unchangeable? In the Bible the primary characteristic of God is that He remains faithful—faithful to His people, faithful to His covenant given long ago to Abraham and Sarah, faithful to His promise to have and to hold from this day forward and forevermore. The biblical God may change in other ways, but He never changes toward us. His promise remains. He is good to His word.

The Bible has a special term for this faithfulness. It is *hesed*. It means a love that is dependable, determined, resolute; a love that creates worth in others; a love that reconciles; a love that loves the unlovely. It is a steadfast love that endures forever.

Hesed is not just another word about God. It is the very heart of God. It is who God is.

It is the one gift you need for your life together. It is the gift all creatures received when He established marriage in the first place. It is a gift He has given us, your families and friends, and now we pass it on to you—a bit tarnished, a bit tempered, but enduring forever.

Real Love, Real People…What an Idea!
James G. Cobb

The Epiphany season most always hits around that great American tradition we call the President's State of the Union Address. Many of us do tune in to listen to a special speech. It is interesting to hear when the applause moments come and later, to listen to various commentators act as scorekeepers, reminding us of how many times the President's speech was interrupted with applause. It is curious too, as a spectator, to watch the other dynamics—when the words and visions are met with division where one side of the house breaks into applause and the other side sits in stony silence. And there is yet a third reaction sometimes: negative head-shaking in outright opposition to what has been said or proposed. There may even burst forth some words, images, and ideas that are prophetic when real truth is told. In that moment, how difficult it is for the truth to be told and to feel it attack or crack or wound our own little worldviews.

It is reported that Abraham Lincoln once made a speech before a huge audience and was greeted with loud and long applause. As he was leaving the podium, a man said, "That was a great speech Mr. President; listen to how they enjoyed what you said!" Lincoln, in his usual self-deprecating manner, responded, "I am kept humble by the fact that the crowd would be twice as large if I were here to be hanged." Sometimes history does write a grand summation for those who speak what they believe to be true no matter what it takes. Sometimes there is a prophetic message that "shakes the foundation" and causes controversy, so much so that it produces discomfort and disquiet.

Our gospel text (Luke 4:21–30) for today does "shake the foundations." Jesus, in his first sermon in his hometown of Nazareth jolts the crowd with his proclamation that the prophecies of Isaiah are now fulfilled in him...today, this very day! As listeners to a "good sermon," the congregation at first takes these words from Jesus, at least through verse 22. The text says that at this point, "all spoke well of him and were amazed at the gracious words that came from his mouth." But, by verse 28, the mood and reactions had so shifted that we read this: "When they had heard this, all in the synagogue were filled with rage." And they got up, nudged him toward the edge of town, led him to the brow of a hill and were about to hurl him off a cliff. If Jesus had ended his sermon with verse 21 and said "Amen," they would have all shaken his hand and said, "Good sermon, Pastor." Instead, five verses later, his listeners were ready to destroy him. What had happened?

God became specific! God knew their hearts. They could at first dismiss what Jesus had to say because he was a hometown boy. They would like to see him work a miracle or two as he had performed in other places. Jesus cuts to the chase and speaks the truth, "No prophet is accepted in his hometown." Then he goes on to illustrate with two specific stories. Once upon a time, there were many widows in Israel, but a prophet named Elijah was sent to a widow in a foreign town, Zarephath in Sidon. Jesus tells another story: Once upon a time, there were many lepers in Israel, but Elisha cleansed a foreigner named Naaman from Syria. And these are the two stories Jesus told. And they all got the point. The movement of God and all that Jesus had spoken and would do was headed into, but also beyond, Israel. The God now set loose in Jesus would be to all the world. This embodied good news would be to all the world and would particularly embrace the outsider, the foreigner, the "least likely," the outcasts, tax collectors, prostitutes, all sinners, even the hated Romans. And therefore, for daring to say such outlandish things, Jesus was near death this day and would be brought to death later, at his crucifixion. Jesus gave specific illustrations of love and grace and mercy. When he became specific, he was in trouble.

We also listen in to other scripture readings and often do so with generic hearing. How many think that 1 Corinthians 13 is about "love in general"? Saint Paul, after listing various gifts that have been given for the upbuilding of the body of Christ, celebrates the particular gifts and talents given to each person; but then he speaks and says, "But I will show you a still more excellent way." He will illustrate that love is the most excellent and wondrous gift of all, not in some general, generic way, but with some specific illustration. Illustrations are contained in words like: patience, kindness, not envious or boastful or arrogant or rude; not insisting on its own way; not irritable or resentful; never rejoicing in wrongdoing, but rejoicing /delighting in the truth. Love is the most excellent way.

A woman visited a small-town newspaper editor hoping to sell him some poems she had written. The crusty old editor asked, "What are your poems about?" "They're about love," gushed the woman. The editor settled back in his chair and said, "Well, read me a poem. The world could use a lot more love."

The poem she read was filled with moons and Junes and other sticky sentiments, and it was more than the editor could take. "I'm sorry," he said, "but you just don't know what love is about. It's not moonlight and roses. It's sitting up all night at a sickbed or working extra hours so the kids can have new shoes. The world doesn't need your brand of poetical love; it needs some good old-fashioned practical love."

From the cartoon strip *Peanuts,* Charlie Brown speaks the difference between general and specific love when he proclaims, "I love humankind; it's just people I can't stand." When love goes specific, then it is raw and real and radical. It finds specificity for caring, serving, and giving. God's love for us is taken, giftwrapped in swaddling clothes, and laid in a manger. God's love for us goes specifically in a person who speaks, acts, teaches, gives up his life in death for us and for all the world. God wraps the gift in a word we come to call *grace.* Grace is a gift. Grace is a gift given freely when we deserve nothing, and grace usually is shocking in both its surprise and its specificity.

The "Dear Abby" column had a story of a young woman named Amy Mulrooney, who wrote in trying to locate a stranger who had helped her in a busy airport in the state of Washington. She had flown to Pullman for an admissions interview at Washington State University, School of Veterinary Medicine. Before she departed on her trip, she made reservations for a rental car and a motel room. She had everything planned, hoping to have a couple of hours of peace and quiet in her motel room before her important interview. At the airport, Amy went to the rental car agency intending to pay with a credit card, but the card was rejected. She had made her payment to clear the card some days before, thought it would clear, but it didn't. She had no way to pay for the car or the room. She wrote that she stood at a pay telephone crying into the receiver as she told her story to a roommate back home, hundreds of miles away. While she cried on that phone, she said a man came up, handed her a hundred-dollar bill and disappeared in the crowd. She was too stunned to speak or ask who he was or why. He just quickly disappeared. She wrote her story, hoping to tell someone out there that she made her interview, got in, was immersed in her studies at school and would never forget the anonymous gift. She wanted someone, the anonymous person, to know of her gratitude.

On a particularly hard day, I had had both hospital visits and a funeral. Dressed still in a clerical collar, I pulled into a drive-through fast-food restaurant to make a quick order. At the cashier's window, the person said, "Your meal was paid for already by the car in front of you; have a nice day." I have no idea who did the surprising and unexpected gifting. These are moments of grace...love gone specific, anonymous. This is grace, out-of-the-blue, undeserved, surprising, a gift full of delight.

Albert Schweitzer once was asked to name the greatest person in the world. The old and revered doctor said, "The greatest person in the world is some unknown individual in some obscure corner of the earth who at this very hour has gone in love to be with another person in need." This is the most excellent way urged upon us by Saint Paul and compelled by the gospel of Jesus Christ. There is a scandal set loose when the gospel becomes specific.

These are wondrous and exciting times around our congregations. I know this congregation that began a soup kitchen, but it is called a "lunch ministry," because it is the work of the gospel set loose in our world to meet the hunger needs of the local community. Many bring some food to supply the kitchen; it is as holy an offering as our tithes and gifts offered at the altar. Many give time to prepare and cook and set up and welcome guests and clean up after a day of serving. And some love and grace go out to some part of our community we call "marginalized," those who are hungry and are sometimes dirty or suspicious or awkward and unknowing of manners and etiquette. In our churches, some children each week are taught stories about Jesus and some songs are sung. This is a more excellent way than sleeping in, missing the fellowship of brothers and sisters in Christ, and ignoring or slighting the gospel. Our congregation engages in work to build a Habitat for Humanity home. This is a more excellent way than keeping monies and energies to ourselves and hoarding life into our own wishes and desires. Through the week in so many of our congregations, church councils and committees meet and plan;

many give the gifts of time and administration, gifts of listening and caring to one another and for the sake of the whole world, and this is a more excellent way!

The Bible has been studied in many of our churches. This is a more excellent way. Some take this more excellent way into jobs and workplaces and try to serve with more patience and kindness and caring than we may ever get back in equal measure, and this is a more excellent way. Some students try to avoid or mediate conflicts or talk through problems with friends and offer gifts of listening, reflection, companionship, and compassion, and this is a more excellent way.

Year after year, in Epiphany's season, we may never know the "state of the union" from the speech we may or may not hear. But this thing we know: The state of the Kingdom is secure, for it is in the hands of God. For in God's kingdom there is the more excellent way of love and grace abounding without end... and without regard for status or standing, without regard for knowledge or power or prestige or any of the illusions and deceits we so pursue in our world, chasing them sometimes feverishly into a lengthening twilight of our years. Thanks be to God that the love of our Lord Jesus Christ is always shown in specific ways, often in scandalous and surprising ways to each of us. And do not be too surprised if strangers and outsiders come in. And do not be too surprised if the undeserving receive great compassion and forgiveness and love and grace. For that is the way of Jesus. He said things like this would happen, and he continues to see to it that they do. For his way of love is most excellent.

Amen.

Funeral Sermon for Glennie Iverson, 1919–1999

Robert Dahlen

Dear friends in Christ, grace to you and peace from God our Father and our Lord and Savior, Jesus the Christ. Amen and Amen.

This afternoon, I want to talk with you about the lesson I read from Saint Paul's first letter to the church at Corinth.

Chapter thirteen is often called the love chapter, and more often than not it's a chapter read at weddings. Well, Glennie never married, today we're not here for a wedding, and I'm not going to talk about love for a little while. Instead, I invite you to think about these verses from the close of the chapter. Paul writes to you and to me:

> Now we see in a mirror dimly, but then face to face.
> Now I know in part; then I shall understand fully, even
> as I have been fully understood (1 Cor. 13:12, RSV).

Paul speaks to us about our life today and says it's as if we were looking in a mirror dimly. We see and understand ourselves as if straining to see through a stained, foggy, streaked mirror. And we're not quite sure of what we see. Paul talks to us about knowing in part. We know and understand only just part of the story. And it's frustrating.

As you and I look back on Glennie's life and think now about his death, there is so much we can't quite figure out. There are so many unanswered questions. We know bits and pieces, we see dimly, we know in part.

Yesterday, I called my father and told him that Glennie had died. As you know, my family and the Iverson family share cousins. My father remembers how when he was a boy, his family would come up here and visit. He would play with his Dahlen cousins, and the Iverson and Johnson kids would be there too. And like so many of his generation, like Glennie and his cousin Olaf, my father went to war. My father and Glennie both ended up wearing a Red Cross during the war; Glennie served as a medic with the Army in North Africa and Europe. My father ended up as a Navy Hospital Corpsman, serving with a Marine invasion force in the south Pacific. They cared for the wounded and buried the dead.

As I talked with my father, I told him that I had seen Glennie's discharge papers. This medic earned six Bronze Stars for meritorious service in combat. My father's response was simple, "Then he went through hell." After that he was very quiet. And I'm old enough not to press things. Sometimes an old veteran's silence speaks volumes. It is enough to know part of the story–leave it at that.

Glennie's life is hard to sort out. There are contradictions so deep that I don't know if we want to sort through it all. Here we have this man surrounded by family. He lived in the same house with his parents for most of his life. Brothers and sisters, cousins and their kids were always there. They worked together, made music together, hunted and trapped together. Yet he was so very isolated, separate, alone, wrestling with his own demons and addictions, acting out in ways that made sense to no one. His last years were spent sitting in his chair, eating TV dinners at room temperature. There was no need to cook them, just set them on the counter to thaw. Can you explain all this? I can't. Right now I don't want go to those places. As the apostle says, "Today we see in the mirror dimly...today we know in part."

But the message of the Bible, the message of Saint Paul in this chapter will not leave us in the fog. No, the message of this chapter is this: Even if today we look in the mirror dimly, there will come a time when we will see clearly, face-to-face. Even if today we can barely make any sense of the story, there will come a day when we will understand it all, even as we have been fully understood. And that day, dear friends in Christ, is yours and mine in Christ Jesus raised from the dead.

There are times when the personal lives of those who gave us the Bible come crashing through and stare us full in the face. This chapter from Paul's first letter to the Corinthians is one of those places. Think about what Paul says here, "Now I know in part—the day is coming when I will understand fully, even as I have been fully understood...even as I have been fully understood." What does he mean here? Well, think about his life.

Paul was not one of the first to follow Jesus. No, he was a very proud, well-educated, almost arrogant man, who sought to destroy the church. Paul, you remember, stood as coatrack when Saint Stephen was put to death. Then with papers from the religious authorities, he sought to lead others to that same spot. Paul had blood—the blood of the faithful—on his hands. But our Lord stopped him in his tracks and called him from being the great persecutor of the church to be the great preacher of God's grace. As he looked back on his life, Paul came to see that God understood him in ways deeper and more gracious than he understood himself. God knew Paul in full. The rage, the hatred, the fear, the isolation, the addictions, the pain...no doubt about it, Gods knows it in full. And still, God called this man Paul from his sin, blinded him with grace, and brought him to new life in Christ.

We do not come here today because we know everything there is to know about Glennie. We do not even come here today because we know and understand ourselves. No! Instead, we come here today, we come to this place, we carry this body to an open grave, because we trust that our Lord is faithful. The God who called Paul to speak of love calls us to do the same. So now is the time to open 1 Corinthians 13 and speak of love.

The gospel story is simple. It says that a Jewish carpenter, teacher, and healer was betrayed by friends and died on a Roman cross. He was buried in a borrowed tomb, and God in love raised Jesus from the dead. Our Lord was raised from the dead so that Mary and Salome, Peter and Paul, James and John, and all the rest might tell others of God's love in Christ. He was raised so that you might know of a love so deep that it defeats even the powers of death. And all this happened so that we might face days like today, a day when the power of what we don't know or understand seems so very strong. God in love for you and for me and for Glennie gives us this gospel so that even as we face this death we might have new life in Him.

Love. "If I speak in the tongues of men and of angels, but have not love...I am nothing." What kind of love are we talking about? We're not talking simply about your love for your brother and uncle Glennie. We're not talking of Glennie's love for you. No! We're not talking about human love at all. Instead, we look to the one raised from the dead and ponder the love of God, which passes all human understanding. We cling to this love, which promises to wipe the mirror clean, and which says that we shall in Christ understand, even as we have been fully understood. We're talking about the love that forgives sinners and raises the dead.

Even so, "Amen, come Lord Jesus."

Epiphany 4, 1998

Fritz Foltz

The Church at Corinth was a lot like the modern American church: split into many denominations; living among many other religions; asking questions about the rights of women, the definition of adultery, the ingredients of a proper diet, the problems of drunkenness, the appropriate place for sex. The situation Paul confronted must have been as bizarre as those on our talk shows. He was asked if Christian freedom meant a man could live with his stepmother as his wife.

We read 1 Corinthians 13 as a beautiful poem about love. It was actually part of a tough argument against those who insisted all Christians had to be Pentecostal. Paul taught tongue-speaking is not essential for everyone, but love is, and suggested their attitude was not loving. "Even if you speak in the tongues of angels, as you claim you do, if you do not live in love, you have no place in the kingdom of God. You are like a clanging cymbal in an orchestra, a very minor often irritating instrument" (author's translation). A piece of music based on the cymbal part would be just meaningless noise.

Some Christians still argue all Christians must be tongue speakers, but most of us apply Paul's argument to other problems, such as the political crisis that has obsessed our nation for the past two weeks, dealing with President Bill Clinton and an intern, Monica Lewinsky.

My daughter-in-law reports that her graduate education course at Penn State began debating this crisis as a controversial political issue, arguing whether the charges were contrived or real. Soon they agreed it did not matter if the charges were false or true; having them blasted into our living rooms via television severely damaged the society and especially our young children. These teachers sadly began to discuss how they could help children develop decent role models in our society.

Christians also need to cry out that this is not what we mean when we speak of love. Love is about leaders serving people, especially the weak, not about political parties obsessed with gaining power and searching out weaknesses of other parties. Love is mutual sharing of yourself and your possessions, especially with the weak, not the strong using their power to seduce the weak.

Paul claims no spiritual gift is for the benefit and power of the individual. All spiritual gifts are to be shared for the building up of the whole community. No spiritual gift is useful unless it is used in love. Even if you have the knowledge to understand everything God understands, you are nothing if you do not use this in love. Even if you have enough faith to move mountains, even if you are so charitable you give away every last one of your possessions, even if you suffer death for your beliefs or sell your self into slavery so your family has enough money to feed themselves, you are nothing in the kingdom of God if you do not do this in love.

That means the goal of Christianity is not individuals' passing a test to get into heaven. The goal is loving community. Everything else is just a means to this end. When God's loving community is established, everything else will pass away. We shall no longer need healing, for there will no longer be sickness or death. We shall no longer need faith, because we shall see God face-to-face. We shall no longer need worship or churches or Bible or theology, because we shall all know God completely. But we shall still need love, because the kingdom of God is a loving community.

Love is not power insisting on its own way. Love is patient, kind, not envious or boastful or arrogant or rude, not irritable or resentful.

This does not mean love puts up with anything for the sake of unity and peace. Love does not rejoice in wrongdoing, but in the truth. When we say love bears all things, we do not mean it puts up with abuse. We mean it endures in spite of everything thrown at it. There is nothing love cannot face and handle.

So in the current situation we can still proclaim with a deep sadness, "Render unto Caesar what is Caesar's," but we make very clear that what we have been seeing and hearing is not in any way related to what we mean by loving community.

Love is about giving, not taking. It is not about what I want, but what the community needs. The strong give to the weak. The strong do not take from the weak.

Love can be trusted by every person in the community. For the past two weeks we have heard all sorts of excuses for adultery—"He loves other people so much, it is just to be expected." Jimmy Carter was right. Jesus said adultery was even to lust in one's heart.

Love is about character, not feeling. Feelings come and go. Character remains. Good character controls feelings for the sake of the group. Good character can love even enemies. Good character knows Beauty and the Beast had it right. We do not love people because they are beautiful. We love them and make them beautiful.

Love is based on role models. God gave us one when Christ died for us while we were sinners, enemies, nobodies. All Christians are called to be role models, because we are all signs that humans can live in a loving community.

Many in our world believe the Christian message is childish, foolish. Paul begins the letter to the Corinthians reporting that even then society regarded the Christian message as foolish. It seems to me what we have heard and seen in the past two weeks demonstrates it is locker-room talk and actions that are adolescent, instant gratification that is childish, and an obsessive spying on other people that is foolish. "When I was a child, I spoke like a child, I thought like a child, I reasoned like a child. When I became an adult, I put an end to childish ways."

Love for Mature Adults Only

Ken Gibble

As someone who has "officiated" at more weddings than I care to remember—more than thirty years' worth of weddings—I have sometimes wondered if, on the day of the wedding, anyone is paying attention. I mean, with all the fuss about the bride's lovely gown and who's got the rings and will the flower girl panic, nobody seems to notice what this occasion is really about. It's about a promise, a vow, a covenant unto death. The language of the marriage covenant isn't afraid to say that word—*death*.

Right in the middle of this happy event, right at the very beginning of marriage, is a reminder that love between marriage partners includes the end: "till death do us part." If that isn't a sobering thought, I don't know what is.

Something else that deserves sober attention is the scripture often read during the wedding ceremony: 1Corinthians 13, or, as it is often called, "the love chapter." This chapter was written by the apostle Paul to members of the Corinthian church. The church in Corinth was troubled by deep divisions. There were factions, with one group claiming Paul as their leader, another group insisting that Peter was the leader, and a third group saying that a man named Apollos was the one they should follow.

The Corinthians were also plagued by disputes about religious practices. Those who had grown up in the Jewish faith thought that everyone in the church should not eat certain kinds of food. Those who weren't Jews thought that was nonsense. In Corinth, the rich members of the church were inconsiderate of those who were poor. At fellowship meals, the wealthy members arrived first and helped themselves to the food and drink. In fact, some of them helped themselves to the wine so liberally that they got drunk. And by the time the members of the church who were working people got there, hardly anything was left on the table. Besides all this, there were disputes about sexual behavior, about whether a believer should be married or single, about the role of women in the church, about what should happen in the worship services. In short, the Corinthian church was a royal mess. And Paul, who had been hearing reports about this state of affairs, decided to write a letter to straighten things out.

What approach did Paul take to this chaos? Well, in his letter, he used not just one approach, but a variety of approaches. He coaxed them, he scolded them, he praised them, he prayed for them, he threatened them, he pleaded with them. He offered advice that was sometimes general, sometimes very specific. And when at last he addressed the matter of spiritual gifts, he decided to compare their situation to the human body. Think of it this way, Paul said. The human body has many parts—ears, eyes, hands, feet. And all the parts are necessary, even though each part has a different function. And that's the way it is in the church, which is the body of

Christ. You can't all be teachers or healers or helpers, Paul told them. Some of you are well-educated, some of you speak with great eloquence, some of you have a wonderful spirit of generosity. Every person's gift is important. You can't do it alone; you need each other. To use Paul's exact words: "There are varieties of gifts, but the same Spirit" (1 Cor. 12:4, NRSV). That quotation comes from the twelfth chapter of Paul's letter. And that chapter ends with these words: "And I will show you a still more excellent way" (12:31, NRSV). Those words are the introduction to the love chapter.

Paul does not write about love in general. Nor is his description of love the kind of thing you find on Valentine cards. It isn't love according to love songs you hear on the radio or see in the movies. Paul is not writing about "falling in love." Paul is writing about the kind of love needed by people who sometimes have a difficult time getting along with each other. It's love for mature adults only. That phrase, "for mature adults only," has a particular meaning in our day. It's a warning that the contents of a book or magazine or movie are sexually explicit. It's an appropriate warning. Such materials are not for children. But neither is the kind of love Paul wrote about. "When we were children," said Paul, "we thought and reasoned as children do. But when we grew up, we quit our childish ways." It takes mature adults to handle *agape* love–love that is kind and patient, that is not rude or selfish or resentful. It's the kind of love that simply isn't present when a young man and young woman stand in front of the minister on their wedding day. The love they know about is love based primarily on feeling– and a wonderful feeling it is, make no mistake. There's nothing quite like it in all the world–to feel desired and treasured by another person. But it's basically child's love, love untested by time and by the bumpy ride we call life.

And that is why, in a wedding service, we remind the couple, and we remind ourselves, that love for mature adults is not based on feelings. It is based on covenant–a solemn promise in the sight of God to be committed to each other, come what may. It's why we ask the couple to promise to hang in there, for better or for worse, for richer or for poorer, in sickness and in health, all the way to the grave. But remember, Paul, writing his love chapter to the Corinthians, did not have a marriage ceremony in mind. In fact, just a few chapters previously Paul wrote that he wished all his Christian friends at Corinth would be as he was—that is, unmarried. Isn't it ironic that we use Paul's words about love at weddings, when Paul recommended against weddings?

Paul intended his words about love for people in the church, who have promised to love the Lord and to love one another. It's a "till death do us part" vow. It is a covenant made in the presence of God, just like a marriage covenant. And there is no fine print that says the people who take this vow have to love only the people who agree with them about the church budget or who like the same kind of music in worship that they do or who are easy to get along with. There is no escape clause that says they don't have to stick with it anymore if they don't like the pastor or if somebody says something to offend them.

Mature love, love that is Christlike, does not insist on its own way. And if you have mature love, you don't restrict it to the people you enjoy spending time with. Jesus didn't say to his disciples: I want you to like one another. He said: "Love one another as I have loved you" (John 15:12, NRSV). And how does Jesus love? He loves fully, completely, unconditionally. His was a love that went to the cross, not just for his friends, but for his enemies as well. "Love one another," says Jesus, "as I have loved you." "Well," you say, "that's very nice, but I can't love that way. I'm just not up to it." And my answer to that is, "Of course you aren't. Neither am I." But we aren't told, we aren't asked, to do it on our own. We ask God to do it with us and for us and through us. That's why, when we receive new members into the church and when we join together a man and woman in marriage, we always pray for God to give them the strength to fulfill their vows, to help them love as mature adults do. With people like you and me, it's impossible. But with God, as Jesus said, "all things are possible" (Mk. 10:27, NRSV).

Nearly every time the love chapter is read—in worship, at weddings—the very next verse is not read. It's the verse that begins the next chapter, chapter 14. But it should be read, because it's Paul's final word on the matter. Paul says, "You must want love more than anything else." That's the Jerusalem Bible translation. But I like even better Eugene Peterson's translation *(The Message):* "Go after a life of love as if your life depended on it–because it does." It does indeed.

Fidelity and Love

William J. Gohl, Jr.

Chris and Sherry, dear friends, sisters and brothers, grace to you and peace from God our Creator and from our Savior, Jesus Christ. Amen.

Fidelity means faithfulness. Fidelity means keeping the promises you make, even when you don't feel like keeping them. Fidelity means hanging in there with the other, even when it isn't very convenient or comfortable to do so. Fidelity means trusting that God who brought you together and established you as husband and wife did not make a mistake.

The Lutheran church does not define marriage as a covenant of love, but rather as a covenant of fidelity. We may be Lutherans, but we're not altogether stupid. We know that the concept of love in our society is so wishy-washy, so highly associated with how you feel, that any marriage based on that sort of love will last only as long as the feelings last. When the time comes that you happen not to feel very loving toward the other, well, that's it. The marriage is over. Let's get a divorce.

But you know what? When marriage is based on fidelity, when you are faithful, love will be close at hand. Romantic love, yes, at times. But a much deeper love as well. A deeper love that takes its pattern from God's love for the world and for us in Jesus Christ. A deeper love that is willing to lay down its life, if need be, to keep faith with God and with neighbor. A deeper love that is symbolized by that cross on the altar right now, as it reaches out its arms to you to unite you in a few minutes as husband and wife, the cross that reaches out its arms to send you out as a new family into the world.

In our lesson this afternoon from the thirteenth chapter of First Corinthians, Saint Paul provides us with a beautiful picture of love in a covenant rooted in fidelity. Love is patient and kind…Love bears all things, believes all things, hopes all things, endures all things…Love is not jealous or boastful…arrogant or rude…irritable or resentful.

It warms our hearts to hear love described in this way. Here is the very ideal of love set forth in some of the most beautiful language ever written.

But we need to be careful at this point. Before we get teary-eyed over the idea of perfect love, we need to remember that what you and I actually experience in real life is not this sort of love at all. In our relationships with others we are not always patient and kind, bearing all things. Seldom do we make it through a day without being jealous or boastful, arrogant or rude, irritable or resentful. The love Paul describes may be what we would like to experience, or at least what we would like to think we experience. But the truth is that not one of us embodies that sort of love for very long.

There is a big gap between the perfect love Paul describes and the imperfect love we practice. When we realize that, we can become frustrated and angry. If what we have in these words about love is an ideal, then we must soberly admit that none of us measures up to this ideal for very long. These words of Paul's are therefore not encouraging at all, but rather, discouraging. They remind us of what we are not, rather than what we are. Paul is giving us bad news, not good news. Why in the world would we read these words at a wedding if they only serve to show how inadequate we really are?

The answer is quite simple. What Paul is describing is not our love, but God's love for us and all the world in Jesus Christ. It is Jesus who is patient and kind. It is Jesus who bears all things, believes all things, hopes all things, endures all things. It is Jesus who is not jealous or boastful, arrogant or rude, irritable or resentful. In other words, it is Jesus who embodies the love Paul is describing. We fall short of the ideal, but Jesus doesn't. We miss the mark of perfect love, but God's love is always on target. We are imperfect, but God is perfect. Therefore, our hope is not in some fairy-tale fantasy about our perfect love for God and neighbor; our hope is in the concrete reality of God's perfect love for all the world in the new covenant made through Jesus Christ.

So, you see, this passage Paul wrote about love is extremely appropriate for a wedding after all, as long as it is understood as a description of God's faithful love and not our own.

Chris and Sherry are now entering a lifelong covenant of marriage. Their marriage does not depend on their ability to love each other perfectly all the time. It depends on fidelity toward each other and faith in God's ability to love them perfectly, even in those moments when their love for each other is weak. There will be dented fenders, miscommunication, and difficulties adjusting to each other. There will be frustrations, doubts, and disappointments. There will be times when the burden of life together will be heavy and the responsibility of managing a household will be cumbersome. If the success of their marriage depends on Chris and Sherry's always feeling perfect love, twenty-four hours a day, seven days a week, for the rest of their lives, there is little hope for success at all. But the good news is that the success of their marriage does not depend on them alone, but on God's ability to work in, with, and through them. On God's ability to bring pardon where there is injury, reconciliation where there is discord, hope where there is despair, joy where there is sadness. The good news is that the perfect love of God can sustain them amid all the imperfections of daily life together. For it is that perfect love of God that brought them into existence. It is that love that flowed through parents, families, teachers, and friends to nurture them along the way. and it is that same love of God that allowed them to fall in love with each other and to arrive at this, their wedding day.

Christian marriage is this: simply living each day by faith, faithfulness toward each other, faithfully allowing yourself to be loved by God in, with, and through each other. It is acknowledging that while no husband or wife is perfect, each husband and each wife is good enough, by the grace of God.

Chris and Sherry, if you want to see God, look at how God is reflected to you in the life and love, the grace and mercy of each other. If you want God to touch you, let your partner touch you on God's behalf. If you want to feel the presence of God, then feel the simple human warmth of the life companion God has placed beside you. If you want to experience the power and majesty of God, then gaze into the mystery of each other's existence. If you want to live with God, then live in fidelity with each other and forgive each other. And if you want to love God in return, love each other. Each of you is God's connection with the other. And through your partnership as husband and wife, your marriage is also one of God's most important connections with all the world.

Chris and Sherry, we rejoice with you this day as you embark on life together as husband and wife. All of your past is received, accepted, and forgiven, and all of your future is open, because of God's love, God's perfect love for you. We rejoice with you this day as you enter a covenant of marriage based on faithfulness and fidelity—a covenant rooted in God's love—a covenant characterized by the passionate sacrifice of self for the sake of the other. We rejoice with you this day as you become a new family in the life of the world: bold to claim the promise of God's love for you each day on Earth, until that day comes when you see God face-to-face, and love is perfected in you eternally.

Amen.

Without Love, I Am Nothing
Billy Graham

Recent events give some indication of the tremendous need for revival in our time. All across the nation reports are coming in that this revival may be on the way. Hundreds and thousands of people are turning to Jesus Christ. God is moving in strange and wondrous ways.

When the eternal statistics are read, perhaps we will find that during this period more people came to Jesus Christ than during any previous period in the history of all Christendom. In our own meetings we have seen many people come to Christ. During the past three years we have had the privilege of reaching more people for Christ and seeing larger crowds than we have ever seen before. We give all the glory and all the praise to God. We are praying that this next year we will see thousands more swept into the kingdom of God. I believe it is the only hope of this hour.

This Is the Hour to Show Love!

As we see a world that is sick, pained, confused, and bewildered, we believe that this is the hour for the church to speak out. This is the hour for the church to show forth the love and grace of God! This is the hour for the world to hear Christ saying through the church, "I am the way, the truth, and the life" (Jn. 14:6).

There is something that Jesus said that I want you to think about. Jesus said to those who followed Him: "By this shall all men know that ye are my disciples, if ye have love one to another" (Jn. 13:35, KJV).

That verse of scripture is tremendously important at this hour in American history. In another part of the Bible we find the same thing stated by John: "Beloved, let us love one another: for love is of God; and every one that loveth is born of God, and knoweth God. He that loveth not knoweth not God; for God is love. In this was manifested the love of God toward us, because that God sent His only begotten Son into the world, that we might live through Him. Herein is love, not that we loved God, but that He loved us, and sent His Son to be the propitiation for our sins" (1 Jn. 4:7–10, KJV).

In Love with Each Other

The Bible declares that we who follow Jesus Christ should be just as much in love with each other as God was in love with us when He sent His Son to die on the cross. I want you to see what it means to love as God loves, because the Bible says, "God is love" (1 Jn. 4:16).

The basic attribute of God is holiness, but love is another basic attribute of God. It is a part of God's nature to love, and all who know Jesus Christ as Savior also have this supernatural love shed abroad in their hearts by the Holy Spirit. The greatest demonstration of the fact that we are Christians is that we love one another.

In 1 Corinthians 13, we have first a description of a man who does not possess love. The apostle Paul says, "Though I speak with the tongues of men and of angels, and have not love, I am become as sounding brass or a tinkling cymbal."

In other words, suppose I could speak with the oratory of a William Jennings Bryan. Suppose I could speak with cryptic language like Churchill. Suppose I could speak with the power of Roosevelt, in which he used to sway an entire nation. Suppose I could sing like Caruso. Suppose I had a thousand tongues that could speak a thousand languages at the same time. The Bible says all that is nothing, and I am nothing, unless I have this divine, supernatural love that God gives.

The apostle goes on to write, "Though I have the gift of prophecy, and understand all mysteries and all knowledge ...and have not [love], I am nothing." I could be a man of tremendous knowledge; I could understand all the mysteries and all of history and be able to put all the patterns together. I could know the Bible from one end to the other; memorize thousands of verses of scripture. I could be a great Bible teacher; I could even be a preacher from the pulpit–and have not love. I know people in this country who are conservative in their theology–people who would die contending for the inspiration of the Bible–and yet there is so little love. I might know the Bible from Genesis to Revelation, but if I had not love, it would mean absolutely nothing in the sight of God.

I might be a man of great faith. The Bible says that I might have faith so that I could move mountains, but if I have not love, it is nothing. Suppose I could stand here today and say to that mountain, "Move into the sea," and it would move! You would say, "Well, Billy Graham is certainly a man of tremendous faith to pray a mountain into the sea." The Bible says that is absolutely nothing unless my faith is tempered with love.

Giving...with Love

I could be a man of great charity. The Bible says, "Though I bestow all my goods to feed the poor...it profiteth me nothing" unless I have this divine love that God gives. Zacchaeus gave half his goods to feed the poor. There is another man who gave all. I could give everything I have to charity, but if the motive were not divine love, it means nothing in the sight of almighty God.

Here in this country we give billions of dollars away, but sometimes I wonder if our motive is not selfish. We are always asking the other nations and the other people, "What return is America going to get?" The motive of all giving and all charity should be love.

You may plan to give Christmas presents. You may be going to give the poor people something to eat at Christmastime. It is all fine and commendable, but I wonder if you are not doing it to salve your conscience. Or are you doing it because you have actual love for those people? If you have real love, you will not only give at Christmastime, but all year long.

I could also be a man of consuming zeal. Paul continues, "Though I give my body to be burned, and have not [love], it profiteth me nothing." Suppose I were like many Korean pastors in recent decades. Seventeen hundred Korean pastors paid with their blood for their faith in Jesus Christ. Suppose I died at a stake or was shot for my faith in Jesus Christ. You would say, "Billy Graham is a man of consuming zeal. He died as a martyr." God says it is nothing unless I am filled with the love of God.

What a brilliant life this man lived–this mythical man the Bible describes. He was a man of eloquence, knowledge, power, charity, zeal, but the Bible says he was absolutely nothing without love.

God Believes in Love!

What a powerful thing love must be! How much stock God puts in love.

You say, "Well, Billy, what do you mean by love? What is a demonstration of love?" We have it demonstrated in 1 Corinthians 13. This might cut some of us to the heart. It is going to probe down deep, because one thing that the church of Christ in America lacks is the demonstration of love, and Jesus said, "By this shall all men know that ye are my disciples, if ye have love one to another" (John 13:35, KJV).

This love that the Bible is talking about in 1 Corinthians 13 "suffereth long." In other words, it is patient. It is kind, it "envieth not." There is no jealousy in this divine love that God gives. It "vaunteth not itself," makes no parade of itself. It is "not puffed up," gives itself no airs. It is a love that demands humility. It never pushes itself to the top, never tries to promote itself, never tries to advertise itself. It is always in the background, truly humble. The thing that we need in the church today is genuine, old-fashioned humility.

Then the Bible says it "doth not behave itself unseemly." It is never rude, it is always courteous and gracious at every turn. It "seeketh not her own," is never selfish. God looks after you and you are to look after others, the Bible says. It is "not easily provoked," not touchy or irritable. If people have to handle you with kid gloves, have to watch out what they say to you, you don't know anything about this love that God is talking about.

Love Holds Hope for Others

It "thinketh no evil." It never holds a grudge—never has malice. It "rejoiceth not in iniquity, but rejoiceth in the truth." It is never glad when another falls. I know so many Christians today who, when they hear that another Christian has fallen, say, "Isn't that too bad?" but they don't mean it! They are happy that the other Christian has fallen because that places them just a little higher on the ladder of estimation in other people's eyes.

Then the Bible says that this love "beareth all things, believeth all things, hopeth all things, endureth all things." It is slow to expose the evils and faults in others. It is eager to believe the best, and it is always hopeful and optimistic concerning the future. The Bible teaches that love is greater than faith and hope. Love is the greatest thing in all the world.

Love Changes Attitudes and Relationships

I will never forget when Redd Harper came to Christ out in Hollywood. He said that to him the most amazing and thrilling thing after he came to Christ was this fact: "I found that I loved everybody, no matter what race or color or creed they might be. I just wanted to go hug the whole world."

I remember when Stuart Hamblen came to Christ. He said the same thing: "I fell in love with the whole world. There were certain people who had different racial characteristics from myself that I did not like before I was converted, but after I gave my heart to Christ, I fell in love with every one of them."

Only this divine love that God gives will make us love others, and before we have revival in America, we must have that kind of love among God's people.

Have You Received God's Gift of Love?

However, the greatest demonstration of love in all the world was God sending His own Son to die for you. You did not deserve to have Him die for you. You are a sinner!

The Bible says that you know nothing about this love if you are outside of Christ. It is impossible for you to have this divine love, because it is a gift of God only to those who love Christ.

But—God loves you! It makes no difference how deep in the mire of sin and transgression you have gone. God loves you today! He proved it by sending His Son, Jesus Christ, to die for you on the cross.

At this moment you can receive Christ into your heart. God will give you this supernatural love until you love the whole world. That is the solution to the international problems that we face at this hour. It is the solution to your personal problems—to let Christ come in. When Christ comes in, loves comes in and love shines forth.

Going Bald Together

Daniel T. Hans

The church in Corinth did not meet in a glass house where no one threw stones; nor did it consist of people wearing TV smiles and class reunion outfits. The Christians in Corinth were real people with real problems. There were factions and scars, conflicts and confusion in that church. And yet, together, by God's grace, they had a real and promising future. Therefore, Paul offered them words that can speak to any church at any time and place, words that could easily be labeled "the bald truth."

A *U.S. News and World Report* article titled "The Bald Truth" (8/4/97) featured a study done at my undergraduate alma mater, Denison University. The study revealed the following:

> Both men and women—those with hair and those without hair—view bald men as "less physically attractive, less socially skilled, and less socially successful than their (hirsute) counterparts."

That's the bald truth! Given this general impression about bald men, I have wondered why God called me into the ministry of influencing people for the sake of the gospel of Jesus Christ, for I am "follicularly challenged"!

Reference to my own baldness brings us to my secondary text. Having already heard Paul's appeal for love within the church in Corinth, I present another appeal for love that presents a challenge to any church in any time and place. This secondary text comes from the children's book *The Velveteen Rabbit*. You may know the story.

> Once upon a time, a new Velveteen Rabbit was brought into a nursery where there also lived a worn-out, bald, old Skin Horse. At first the little boy of the nursery played with the Velveteen Rabbit daily. But then, as usually happens, the boy soon tired of the rabbit and abandoned it to the closet floor as he pursued more sophisticated toys. One day the Velveteen Rabbit noticed the old Skin Horse sitting nearby on the closet floor and asked: "What is REAL?...Does it mean having things that buzz inside you and a stick-out handle?"
>
> "Real isn't how you are made," said the Skin Horse. "It's a thing that happens to you. When a child loves you for a long, long time, not just to play with, but REALLY loves you, then you become Real."
>
> "Does it hurt?" asked the Rabbit.
>
> "Sometimes," said the Skin Horse, for he was always truthful. "When you are Real you don't mind being hurt."
>
> "Does it happen all at once, like being wound up," he asked, "or bit by bit?"
>
> "It doesn't happen all at once," said the Skin Horse. "You become. It takes a long time. That's why it doesn't

often happen to people who break easily or have sharp edges or who have to be carefully kept. Generally, by the time you are Real, most of your hair has been loved off, and your eyes drop out, and you get loose in the joints and very shabby. But these things don't matter at all, because by the time you are Real you can't be ugly, except to people who don't understand."

"I suppose YOU are Real?" asked the Rabbit. And then he wished he had not said it, for he thought the Skin Horse might be sensitive. But the Skin Horse only smiled.

"The Boy's Uncle made me Real," he said. "That was a great many years ago; but once you are Real you can't become unreal again. It lasts for always."[3]

What congregation and what pastor does not have a desire to be real, to be the people God has created and redeemed us in grace to be! Being real, however, is no easy task.

The wisdom of the Skin Horse reminds us that it doesn't happen overnight and it doesn't happen to people who break easily or have sharp edges or who have to be carefully kept.

The wisdom of the Skin Horse tells us that becoming real takes time spent together, and it involves a shared love that usually leaves at least one of the parties bald!

Here are a few suggestions on how a congregation and a pastor can become real with one another as they love one another's hair off in their shared service to Jesus Christ. For these suggestions I return to my primary text, 1 Corinthians 13.

Paul says: "Love is patient." Patience is the reality test for any pastor and congregation.

If it took God six days to create the world; if it took Israel forty years of wandering in the wilderness to become ready to enter the promised land; if it took Jesus three days to rise from the dead; and if it has taken the church two millennia to get only to where we are today in our witness to God's grace, justice, and righteousness, what makes us think a pastor and congregation can fulfill their calling together in but a few brief years?

Time together is a key to faithful ministry between pastor and congregation.

Stick together, work together, listen to each other, challenge each other, and do this day after day, year after year. Patience with each other is needed to build the kingdom of God's love.

Paul says: "Love does not insist on its own way."

The church today does not need authoritarian leaders who demand that things be done *their* way. Rather, the church needs leadership with authority, authority that arises from following Jesus who is *the way*.

Likewise, pastors today do not need congregations that "break easily or have sharp edges or have to be carefully kept." Nor do pastors need congregations that cling with white knuckles to the old ways of doing things.

Rather, pastors need a family of believers who are open to the leading of God's spirit, who welcome change when change advances the kingdom of God and who continually ask, What is the way of Jesus in this situation?

A real congregation and a real pastor, seeking to go Christ's way of love, moving ahead with a vision of what they can become together in God's grace, can do great things for the kingdom of God.

Paul says: "Love does not rejoice in wrongdoing, but rejoices in the truth."

To be real with one another, we have to be honest with one another. For a pastor and a congregation to be honest with each other means to risk letting their hair down with each other. A congregation should expect great things from its pastor, but the people must never forget that before becoming their pastor, he or she was and still is a human being, a sinner like the rest of them, dependent on grace. A pastor should expect great things from a congregation, but a pastor must never forget that before being baptized into the faith, they were and still are sinners, like that pastor, dependent on grace.

The truth is that each of us is but a hasty, selfish, stupid mistake away from destructive wrongdoing that can hurt all of us. Therefore, truth requires accountability between pastor and congregation. We need to be as truthful with each other about each other as the Skin Horse was truthful with the Velveteen

Rabbit and as Paul was truthful with the folks in Corinth. Not the kind of truthful accountability that looks like a witch hunt; rather, the kind of truthful accountability that looks like one beggar showing another beggar where to find bread.

In their pursuit together of truth in the kingdom of God, congregations and pastors need to do more than just let their hair down with each other; they need to love the hair off each other. God's truth is approached only through God's love. We get into trouble as pastors, as congregations, and as denominations when we separate truth from love, seeking one without the other.

I have been blessed with three congregations so far in my ministry, each of which has loved off some of my hair. My prayer for every pastor and every congregation is that they go bald together.

Patiently, humbly, graciously, learn to love each other's hair off.

Such real love, according to the Skin Horse, "lasts for always."

Such real love, according to Paul, "never ends."

Whose Love?

Thomas Henderson

> Love is patient; love is kind; love is not envious or boastful or arrogant or rude. It does not insist on its own way; it is not irritable or resentful.

Familiar words, aren't they? We often hear Paul's words about love read and see them printed. But have *you ever been able to love* in this way? Have you ever *known* this kind of love? Patient and kind, not resentful, not insisting on its own way. Have you ever experienced this sort of love? Have you ever loved another with a love of this kind?

These words are familiar and dearly loved. But they are also troublesome. Our society has abused and even raped love. The word love has almost become senseless. And the concept of love is sometimes so twisted that it has been robbed of its power. We hear the word used so carelessly that we may wonder what it tells us about another.

There is one characteristic of abusive spouses that seems almost universal. Again and again, we hear stories of the husband who beats his wife without mercy—and does so on a consistent basis. However, after an episode of abuse, he is most likely to become repentant. He is likely to cry and beg for his wife's forgiveness. And he is most likely to declare how deeply and dearly he loves her. In spite of such expressions of love, remorse, and penitence, within a few days he will probably once again batter his wife as viciously as before. His affirmations of love are hollow. His declarations of love lie. For whatever reason, love means something entirely different to him than we would suppose it to mean.

In a sense, love has almost become a hollow and meaningless word. Strangely enough, however, this fact actually makes all the more important Paul's hymn of love.

It's easy to become confused these days about what is most valuable and important. Values are changing so fast! We wake up in the morning and don't know what's still worth our while. I think of my mother's values—the ones she tried to instill in me. Most of those values have now been abandoned by our society. The others are seriously challenged. For instance, Sally Fields notes society's values when she was starring in the television show *Gidget,* many years ago. She was not allowed to show her belly-button in the show! Whether for the better or the worse, in the last half-century our values have changed drastically.

Amid such change, it is good to hear Paul claim *there is something that doesn't change.* Love never ends. But as for prophecies, they will come to an end; as for tongues, they will cease; as for knowledge, it will come to an end. For we know only in part, and we prophesy only in part; but when the complete comes, the partial will come to an end. Of course, Paul was trying to settle some silly disputes among the Christians in Corinth.

They seem to have been consumed with petty squabbling and childish competition. Like children they taunted one another, "My gift is more important than your gift!" And as a result, the congregation was coming apart at the seams. Their so-called community of faith had become teams contesting with one another. So Paul points them to the one thing that is lasting and worthwhile—love.

In that sense this passage is strikingly relevant for our own day. How many of us have not wondered what is lasting and worthwhile? How many of us from time to time get confused in the mayhem of changing values? How many of us have asked—or are still asking—that fundamental question: What's my life for?

But some of us may have a problem with Paul's message. Not that I think love is not lasting or not important. It's certainly clear that Paul was right on this score. What does worry me is how one *practices* this value. What confuses me is whether or not I can *embrace that value through my actions*. Oh sure, it's easy to say theoretically that love is eternal. I can confess my faith that love is the only durable thing in human life. That everything else is going to fade away and there will be nothing left but love. However, what good is *saying* all that, *if I cannot practice love in my daily life?*

Just listen to how Paul describes this love about which he writes. First he tells us what love is: "Love is patient; love is kind." Then he reports what is absent when love is present: "Love is not envious or boastful or arrogant or rude. It does not insist on its own way; it is not irritable or resentful; it does not rejoice in wrongdoing, but rejoices in the truth." And finally he goes back to describing what is characteristic of love: "It bears all things, believes all things, hopes all things, endures all things. Love never ends."

Every time we are envious, resentful, boastful, arrogant, rude, or irritable we are not loving! Every time we insist on our own way or rejoice in wrongdoing, we demonstrate that we are not loving. *These are high standards!* These are tough requirements! Paul sounds like a starry-eyed idealist—a utopian. It sounds like he forgot who we humans are. As a matter of fact, it sounds as if he has forgotten who he is. Remember? In Romans 7:15 he declares, "I do not understand my own actions. For I do not do what I want [for example, love], but I do the very thing I hate."

Paul sets the bar terribly high—so high that he himself may not be able to clear it. Yet it sounds like he expects his readers to practice this kind of love. He urges his readers to "strive for the greater gift," that is, for love. Today the passage probably doesn't quite work that way. Instead of becoming more loving because of these words, most of us hear it read and simply feel guilty. We know our faltering efforts at love are skimpy at best.

If we strive for love but fall short, what is there for us to do? Frank McCourt's father, Malachy, is an example of one who strives to love–strives so very hard–but falls short. As many of you know, Frank McCourt is the subject and author of the book and movie entitled *Angela's Ashes*. Angela, Frank's mother, tries to hold her family together through the agony of life in Ireland during its depression. Her husband is clearly a sincere and devoted father and husband. The difficult and desperate circumstances in which they are forced to live, however, wears Malachy down. He does his best to get a job; he does his best to be a responsible parent. But each time he makes a little money, each time he gets a break, he fails. He ends up at the pub to have a pint or two. He eventually staggers home intoxicated, and the newly earned money has been burned up in booze. He is addicted to alcohol, the only way he knows to survive his terrible life. But his addiction prevents him from enacting his love for his family.

It's easy for us to criticize Malachy, to accuse and condemn him. The terrible thing is that most of us have a similar addiction. Maybe not an addiction to alcohol or drugs. But it may be an addiction to self, to fame, to success, to failure, or simply to the pleasures of life. Addictions that stifle genuine love. Addictions that siphon off all our best intentions, just as they siphoned off Malachy's best intentions. So what do we do? Love is indeed the only lasting value we know. And we cannot find it in ourselves to practice that value on a daily basis. *What do we do?*

For me, Paul's powerful statement of love does two important things. It does indeed provide a value–a virtue–when there seem to be none left. However, it also sends us looking for *the power to love,* looking for a source of love for our lives. In classical Lutheran fashion, these words hammer away at my self-confidence. They finally force me to admit that I cannot live this virtue–at least not consistently.

But must I live this virtue? Must I live it without failure? I think that is not finally the point of Paul's statement of love. He claims that love is the only lasting value. "Love never ends." In fact, it is the most important of all those things we believe endure: "Faith, hope, and love abide, these three; and the greatest of these is love." What Paul doesn't explicitly say, but surely knew, is this: The reason for love's stature is that God is love. Love is the character of God. Love is the essence of the divine. Love never ends because God never ends.

Therefore, God is the source of our love. God is the one who empowers us to love, when our own powers are exhausted. Love is not so much an achievement as it is a gift–a gift from God. The greatest and highest gift God can bestow.

This beautiful and powerful passage points us beyond ourselves. We may think that it directs our attention to our own powers to love. But when we follow that path, we end up not with ourselves but with God. Hiking in the woods, we may intend to take a path that leads us back to our campsite. However, instead, and unexpectedly, we find ourselves standing beneath a beautiful waterfall–far away from where we started and where we intended to be. The love Paul describes is a path that eventually leads us to God's love for us expressed in Christ.

The problem then may not actually be our own unloving character–not our inability to practice love. Sure, that is always a problem for us humans. However, the real problem may be our failure to acknowledge and confess our unloving character. So long as we think that we can of our own power live the love Paul describes here, we are hiding from ourselves. Duping ourselves. And until we recognize that fact, we may not be able to know that God has loved us with a love exactly like what Paul describes here. Perhaps the failure to see ourselves as we really are is one of "the childish ways" Paul says he has put away. And having put it away, he is able to see himself as he truly is and God as God truly is.

God loves us with a patient and kind love. It's a love that bears all things, including our failures and weakness. It is a love that hopes all things for us–the very best of things for us. And it is a love that endures all things with us.

Since God loves us in this way, we can go and love others with a love that comes from God. Not a love we conjure up within ourselves. But a compassion that comes from God through us to others.

A few years ago, a television evangelist made famous a motto with which he closed his show: "God loves you and so do we." It might be more honest to amend that admirable statement to read something like this: "God loves you, and because of God's love, I'm trying my best to do the same."

Wedding Sermon

Michelle A. Holley

Many of us learned a song as children about building houses. Perhaps you too learned it in Sunday school or maybe in vacation Bible school. It goes like this. A wise man built his house upon the rock. House upon the rock. House upon the rock. A wise man built his house upon the rock, and the rains came tumbling down. The rains came down and the floods came up. The rains came down and the floods came up. The rains came down and the floods came up. And the house on the rock stood firm. A foolish man built his house upon the sand. House upon the sand. House upon the sand. A foolish man built his house upon the sand, and the rains came tumbling down. The rains came down and the floods came up. The rains came down and the floods came up. The rains came down and the floods came up. And the house on the sand went splat.

Today a new house is being built. It's not being built out of bricks, boards, or mortar. It's not a house on which property taxes will ever be paid. In fact, we could say it is not just a new house, but a new community that is being built here today in the marriage of Shelley and Tim. A brand new community has its roots in this very special, well-planned time we have set aside to bring these two families together.

Now as the song we started with reminds us, it is very important for a house to have a firm foundation. No one wants to see a house go splat. Shelley and Tim, take a moment to think about the foundation you want for this home you are starting together today. The apostle Paul gives us an idea of a foundation in the reading from First Corinthians that we heard earlier. For Paul the foundation of *all* relationships is love. Love is what binds every relationship together. It is the rock foundation, which builds us up. It is the foundation that undergirds the other gifts we have been given: in our occupations, in our other activities, in our communities, and in our relationships.

It may seem strange to say at a wedding, but the truth is that love as it is presented here is not a feeling. It is not the emotional attraction between a man and a woman. Saint Paul was not suddenly overcome in the middle of his letter by some emotional interlude. What Paul is getting at here is that love is a reality, one that we live in and act in as Christians. Our spiritual gifts, whatever they may be—preaching, teaching, music, listening, caring for others—are founded in love. When love is not present, these gifts from God are useless. As well, love is what we have now and what we will have always. When our spiritual gifts fall away, love will be there. Because love is what our relationship with God is all about, it grounds and directs our relationships in the present. So it is more than love between the two of you; it is about the love God has for both of you and the love you will share with all those you encounter.

Saint Paul does not try to list *every* possible spiritual gift in this passage. He is not trying to cover all gifts, because the variety of gifts can be as various as the diversity of people God has created and the Holy Spirit has endowed. One of the gifts we are given is being in relationship with one another. If we have been given the opportunity to be in a marital relationship with someone and have many gifts to share with them in that relationship, but don't have love, we are noisy gongs or clanging cymbals in our marriage. If we don't employ the gifts of listening and empowering our partners, we gain nothing. Saint Paul wants us to build up the other, so that those we are empowering are able to express their spiritual gifts in healthy ways and be who God has called them to be. Our patience and kindness for our spouse comes from love, no matter how envious, boastful, or right we may feel at the time. Does this mean we always need to be like-minded? No, not at all. The diversity of your relationship will be as much of a blessing and excitement in helping to bring out things in the other as when you agree. As well, when one of you suffers, both of you will suffer. But when one of you receives honor and recognition, you both will share in that honor. This is what building the house of your marital relationship includes. It means living from this active foundation of love.

Yet as we all know, the rains will come tumbling down. Shelley and Tim, there will be stresses and changes in your relationship. Challenges you cannot begin to imagine. Without love we are unable to bear those rains when they come. We are unable to have hope and belief. We are unable to endure the torrential downpour that life on this earth brings. But if your foundation is love, if when everything else is washed away, love remains, your house will stand firm. Because love never ends. God's mercy and faithfulness to you individually and your marriage will stand firm. Solid as a rock. We can recall God's acts of unfailing love for the human family, for the house of Israel, and for all of us in the death of God's own son on the cross. When viewed from the outside, that moment of complete divine love in the cross has seemed foolish, humiliating, and absurd to many people. But we know that it was the most incredible gift of love—victory over death for our eternal lives. And that unfailing love of God will continue long after death parts you.

Probably everyone present here today remembers when one of you was a child. You spoke like a child. Perhaps sang songs about wise and foolish men. Acted like a child. Maybe building little houses in a sandbox or rock pile. Thought and reasoned like a child. Perhaps at one time you thought all you had to say is "I do" to be guaranteed of living happily ever after. Through the experience of living and the love in your communities of families, friends, and church you grew into adults, leaving your childlike ways behind. But in every significant change in our lives, we give birth to a new part of ourselves. In the beginning of this adventure called marriage, you might resort to some of those childlike ways as you try to figure out how to live with one another. However, as you patiently grow into this relationship, you will leave those childlike ways behind.

In a moment when you look into each other's eyes as you say your vows, remember you are seeing God indirectly, as we are all created in God's image. As humans, we experience God in indirect ways with the promise that in God's time we will meet face-to-face.

We thank God for the joy you, Shelley and Tim, have found in each other. And it is in God's constant love that we may employ *all* our spiritual gifts in a life of praise of God, whose loving work alone holds true and endures as a rock-solid foundation forever.

Amen.

Wedding Sermon

J. David Knecht

Saint Paul writes "[Love] bears all things, believes all things, hopes all things, endures all things." That is one tall order for any person if we take the lesson we have just read and apply it to ourselves and ask these questions: Can I bear all things? Can I believe all things? Can I endure all things? Then, before answering, think about your own experiences with your spouse, or if you are single, your parents, your siblings or your significant other. Did you bear all things? Did you believe all things? Did you hope all things? Did you endure all things?

I will not presume to answer these questions for you; I can only tell you of my experience. I do not bear all things. I certainly do not believe all things, nor hope all things, and in the endurance department as well as the height department I come up a bit short. Now, because I do not measure up to this high standard of love, does that mean that I do not have love?

Well, I hope not. Indeed I love my wife very much. I am sure that just about everyone in this room has someone whom they love as well. And just because you or I do not measure up to that perfect standard does not mean that you and I do not have love. What we do not have is perfect love. We have human love, which comes with all the baggage that we bring with it.

For you see, this beautiful lesson about love we just read together from First Corinthians is not about us. It's about the love of God and Jesus; no wonder we can't measure up. We are not God. Jesus had to prove his love for us by going to the cross. Thank the Lord we do not need to do that! Saint Paul reminds us that "we know only in part" and that about this love, "we see in a mirror dimly." Therefore, we do not have all the answers, and none of us has a perfect love. Perfect love belongs to God.

Now to be fair, sometimes we do pretty good; we can be supportive, we can be loving, we can be tolerant, we can be truthful, and we can at least in some part mirror God's love for us in our relationships with each other, and often God's Holy Spirit prompts us to do this. Indeed, that is our hope for Rob and Stephanie's love.

However, we need to be honest with ourselves and realize that sometimes—like 3:00 in the morning after a prolonged discussion, or dare we say argument, with the one whom we love—perfect love is not possible. Sometimes because we are human we will put ourselves first before the one we love. This may be why Paul says that we see in the mirror only dimly. Indeed, Rob and Stephanie will have their peaks and valleys in their marriage just like the rest of us do in our relationships.

So that brings us to why we are here, the most important aspect of this day. Weddings are not festivals where we idealistically celebrate some perfect love that only exists in heaven. No, weddings in the church are much more important. Stephanie and Rob are here to declare their love for each other, and we are here to support them. For you see, Stephanie and Rob are not the only ones making promises today. We are making a promise as well. We are promising to listen to them, to support them, to pray for them, and yes, to love them. That is what this service is all about.

We are telling them by our presence and prayers that we are here for them. I can honestly say that sometimes they will need us, and sometimes we will need their support in our relationships. So prepare for your promise today; be ready to be there for Rob and Stephanie in good times and in bad.

Rob and Stephanie, prepare yourselves for your promises, and be ready to be there for each other in good times and bad. And we will all be praying with you that God and God's Holy Spirit will go with you and guide you, and that the Spirit will prompt us to be there for you, so that you can see reflected in the love of your family and friends, the love that God has for you in Jesus.

Amen.

Toward a Biblical Theology of Love
Lamontte M. Luker

God of course has many attributes. Justice. Righteousness. Exodus 15 even says, "The LORD is a warrior, the LORD is his name." But the attribute that the Christian movement lifted up as preeminent is love. Rabbi Jesus' favorite metaphor for God was loving parent. And Saint John would summarize his rabbi's teaching with the dictum: God is love.

The book in the Old Testament that comes closest to the theology of "God is love" is the Song of Songs, but more of that later. The book that comes second closest is Hosea.

The prophet Hosea, through his marriage, experienced the love of God. He married Gomer, and in their marital bliss they had three children. God told Hosea and Gomer to name their babies with symbolic names that would serve as messages to Israel. Their children were to be, as it were, living sermons for the community about them.

Now, Israel had a problem with monotheism, that is, the worship of the one God of the exodus. They didn't doubt this God's existence. They just didn't have enough faith to believe that he not only could liberate them from all that enslaved them but also could sustain their crops, bless their families, and grant them *shalom*. So they said their creed about the God of Sinai, but went on in their practical lives to worship the baals and asherahs, idols of Canaan.

Gomer and Hosea named their first child *Jezreel*, a nomen with an ambiguous omen. *Jezreel* means "God Sows," and is the name of a very fertile valley, where, however, many bloody battles were fought. Whenever people saw this boy, they would think, "God exists to sow blessing; to cut myself off from this source brings judgment."

Hosea and Gomer's second child was a daughter named *Lo Rukhamah*, "Not Pitied." The word for pity or mercy in

Hebrew comes from the word for womb and relates to God's motherly love. God's love is like a mother's, and it pains her when her children forsake her.

The third child was another boy named *Lo Ami,* "Not My People." It must have pained Mother God to her very soul to name this boy such: Israel, her children, had left her.

And at this point Hosea's wife, Gomer, left him. She went through a series of lovers and fell into prostitution. Meanwhile Hosea raised the kids, but suffered the heart-wrenching angst of a love lost. One day he found Gomer. She had been sold into slavery. With her joyful consent, he paid her ransom, freed her, and brought her home. All was forgiven. They never spoke of it again. Through these events, Hosea experienced the love of God.

Israel, like Gomer, had gone after other lovers. Hosea had experienced the pain that God feels when we leave him. Hosea says to the people,

> Come, let us return to the LORD...After two days he will revive us; on the third day he will raise us up, that we may live before him. Let us know, let us press on to know the LORD; his appearing is sure as the dawn; he will come to us like the showers, like the spring rains that water the earth. (Hos. 6:1–3)

Now, *know* is a pregnant word in Hebrew, because it means to consummate a marriage. God wants us to know God as lover. Intimately, as spouses love. How sure is the dawn? Pretty darn sure! How sure are spring rains? Darn sure! That's God's love for us. But our love is often like a morning cloud, like the dew that goes away early (6:4). Alas! Hosea speaks for God, "I desire steadfast love, intimate knowledge, more than anything else" (6:6, author's translation).

Soon after, he preached a poem describing the father-mother God's love for us:

> When Israel was a child, I loved him, and out of Egypt I called my son. The more I called them the more they went from me; they kept sacrificing to the Baals, and offering incense to idols. Yet it was I who taught Ephraim to walk, I took them up in my arms; but they

did not know that I healed them. I led them with cords of human kindness, with bands of love. I was to them like those who lift infants to their cheeks. I bent down to them and fed them...How can I give you up, Ephraim? How can I hand you over, O Israel?...My heart recoils within me; my compassion grows warm and tender. I will not execute my fierce anger; I will not again destroy Ephraim; for I am God and no mortal, the Holy One in your midst, and I will not come in wrath. (Hos. 11:1–9)

What love. What unconditional love. What forgiving, incomprehensible, and transcendent love is God.

Saint John says, "Beloved, let us love one another; for love is of God, and he who loves is born of God and *knows* God. He who does not love does not know God; *for God is love"* (1 Jn. 4:7–8, RSV). We move here from an attribute of God to life in God; for to love is to know God.

Song of Songs in the Old Testament never mentions the word *God,* only the word *love.* For this book of the Bible, as for First John, to love is to know God, because God is love. The bride sings to her husband, "Set me as a seal upon your heart, as a tattoo upon your arm; for love is strong as death" (8:6, author's translation).

Ruth exemplifies such love when she pledges herself to her mother-in-law:

> Entreat me not to leave you or to return from following you; for where you go I will go, and where you lodge I will lodge; your people shall be my people, and your God my God; where you die I will die, and there will I be buried. May the LORD do so to me and more also if even death parts me from you. (Ruth 1:16–17, RSV)

David expressed this divine love upon the death of his best friend, Jonathan: "Jonathan lies slain upon your high places. I am distressed for you, my brother Jonathan; greatly beloved were you to me; your love to me was wonderful, passing the love of women" (2 Sam. 1:25b–26).

There are several attributes of the Divine that, if our loving mother-father-spouse God so graces us, we might copy. Justice. Righteousness. Warrior for a cause. But the greatest of these is love. To be godly is to be godlike. Hosea discovered this in both directions: loving like God, and learning the love of God. Saint Paul said it best:

> If I speak in the tongues of mortals and of angels, but do not have love, I am a noisy gong or a clanging cymbal. And if I have prophetic powers, and understand all mysteries and all knowledge, and if I have all faith, so as to remove mountains, but do not have love, I am nothing. If I give away all my possessions, and if I hand over my body so that I may boast, but do not have love, I gain nothing. Love is patient; love is kind; love is not envious or boastful or arrogant or rude. It does not insist on its own way; it is not irritable or resentful; it does not rejoice in wrongdoing, but rejoices in the truth. It bears all things, believes all things, hopes all things, endures all things. Love never ends…Faith, hope, and love abide, these three; and the greatest of these is love. (1 Cor. 13)

Our Lord Jesus Christ got into trouble loving. He loved sinners, fishermen, tax-collectors, Samaritans, prostitutes. I'm not saying he loved the sins, but he loved the sinners. More than Hosea who paid the price of Gomer in money, Jesus paid the price for us with his life. So we can sing the Song of Songs: "With great delight I sat in his shadow, and his fruit was sweet to my taste. He brought me to the banqueting house, and his intention toward me was love" (2:3–4).

Sunday Before Lent [4]

Martin Luther

Paul's Praise of Christian Love

Paul's purpose in this chapter is to silence and humble haughty Christians, particularly teachers and preachers. The

Gospel gives much knowledge of God and of Christ, and conveys many wonderful gifts, as Paul recounts in Romans 12 and in First Corinthians 12. He tells us some have the gift of speaking, some of teaching, some of Scripture, exposition; others of ruling; and so on. With Christians are great riches of spiritual knowledge, great treasures in the way of spiritual gifts. Manifest to all in the meaning of God, Christ, conscience, the present and the future life, and similar things. But there are to be found few indeed who make the right use of such gifts and knowledge; who humble themselves to serve others, according to the dictates of love. Each seeks his own honor and advantage desiring to gain preferment and precedence over others.

We see today how the Gospel has given to men knowledge beyond anything known in the world before, and has bestowed upon them new capabilities. Various gifts have been showered upon and distributed among them which have redounded to their honor. But they go unheeding. No one takes thought how he may in Christian love serve his fellow-men to their profit. Each seeks for himself glory and honor, advantage and wealth. Could one bring about for himself the distinction of being the sole individual learned and powerful in the Gospel, all others to be insignificant and useless, he would willingly do it; he would be glad could he alone be regarded as Mister Smart. At the same time he affects deep humility, great self-abasement, and preaches of love and faith. But he would take it hard had he, in practice, to touch with his little finger what he preaches. This explains why the world is so filled with fanatics and schismatics, and why every man would master and outrank all others. Such as these are haughtier than those that taught them. Paul here attacks these vainglorious spirits, and judges them to be wholly insignificant, though their knowledge may be great and their gifts even greater, unless they should humble themselves and use their gifts in the service of others.

To these coarse and mean people he addresses himself with a multitude of words and a lengthy discourse, a subject he elsewhere disposes of in a few words; for instance, where he says (Phil. 2:3–4), "In lowliness of mind each counting other better than himself; not looking each of you to his own things, but each of you also to the things of others." By way of illustration, he would pass sentence upon himself should he be thus blameworthy; this more forcibly to warn others who fall far short of his standing. He says, "If I speak with the tongues of men and of angels."

That is, though I had ability to teach and to preach with power beyond that of any man or angel, with words of perfect charm, with truth and excellence informing my message—though I could do this, "but have not love (charity)," and only seek my own honor and profit and not my neighbor's, "I am become sounding brass, or a clanging cymbal." In other words, "I might, perhaps, thereby teach others something, might fill their ears with sound, but before God I would be nothing." As a clock or a bell has not power to hear its own sound, and does not derive benefit from its stroke, so the preacher who lacks love cannot himself understand anything he says, nor does he thereby improve his standing before God. He has much knowledge, indeed, but because he fails to place it in the service of love, it is the quality of his knowledge that is at fault (1 Cor. 8:1-12). Far better he were dumb or devoid of eloquence, if he but teach in love and meekness, than to speak as an angel while seeking but his own interests. "And if I have the gift of prophecy."

According to chapter 14, to prophesy is to be able, by the Holy Spirit's inspiration, correctly to understand and explain the prophets and the Scriptures. This is a most excellent gift. To "know mysteries" is to be able to apprehend the spiritual meaning of the Scriptures, or its allegorical reference, as Paul does where (Gal. 4:24-31) he makes Sarah and Hagar representative of the two covenants, and Isaac and Ishmael of the two peoples—the Jews and the Christians. Christ does the same (Jn. 3:14) when he makes the brazen serpent of Moses typical of himself on the cross; again, when Isaac, David, Solomon and other characters of sacred history appear as figures of Christ. Paul calls it "mystery"—this hidden, secret meaning, beneath the primary sense of the narrative. But "knowledge" is the understanding of practical matters, such as Christian liberty, or the realization that the conscience is not bound. Paul would say, then: "Though one may understand the Scriptures, both in their obvious and their hidden sense; though he may know all about Christian liberty and a proper conversation; yet if he have not love, if he do not with that knowledge serve his neighbor, it is all of no avail whatever; in God's sight he is nothing."

Note how forcibly yet kindly Paul restrains the disgraceful vice of vainglory. He disregards even those exalted gifts, those gifts of exceeding refinement, charm and excellence, which naturally produce pride and haughtiness though they command the admiration and esteem of men. Who would not suppose the Holy Spirit to dwell visibly where such wisdom, such discernment of the Scriptures, is present? Paul's two epistles to the Corinthians are almost wholly directed against this particular vice, for it creates much mischief where it has sway. In Titus 1:7, he names first among the virtues of a bishop that he be "non superbus," not haughty. In other words that he do not exalt himself because of his office, his honor and his understanding, and despise others in comparison. But strangely Paul says, "If I have all faith, so as to remove mountains, but have not love, I am nothing."

Love the Spirit's Fruit Received by Faith

We hold, and unquestionably it is true, that it is faith which justifies and cleanses (Rom. 1:17, 10:10; Acts 15:9). But if it justifies and purifies, love must be present. The Spirit cannot but impart love together with faith. In fact, where true faith is, the Holy Spirit dwells; and where the Holy Spirit is, there must be love and every excellence. How is it, then, Paul speaks as if faith without love were possible. We reply, this one text cannot be understood as subverting and militating against all those texts which ascribe justification to faith alone. Even the sophists have not attributed justification to love, nor is it possible, for love is an effect, or fruit, of the Spirit, who is received through faith.

Three answers may be given to the question. First, Paul has not reference here to the Christian faith, which is inevitably accompanied by love, but to a general faith in God and his power. Such faith is a gift; as, for instance, the gift of tongues, the gift of knowledge, of prophecy, and the like. There is reason to believe Judas performed miracles in spite of the absence of Christian faith, according to John 6:70: "One of you is a devil."

This general faith, powerless to justify or to cleanse, permits the old man with his vices to remain, just as do the gifts of intellect, health, eloquence, riches.

A second answer is: Though Paul alludes to the true Christian faith, he has those in mind who have indeed attained to faith and performed miracles with it, but fall from grace through pride, thus losing their faith. Many begin but do not continue. They are like the seed in stony ground. They soon fall from faith. The temptations of vainglory are mightier than those of adversity. One who has the truth faith and is at the same time able to perform miracles is likely to seek and to accept honor with such eagerness as to fall from both love and faith.

A third answer is: Paul, in his effort to present the necessity of love, supposes an impossible condition. For instance, I might express myself in this way: "Though you were a god, if you lacked patience you would be nothing." That is, patience is so essential to divinity that divinity itself could not exist without it, a proposition necessarily true. So Paul's meaning is, not that faith could exist without love, but on the contrary, so much is love an essential of faith that even mountain-moving faith would be nothing without love, could we separate the two even in theory. The third answer pleases me by far the best, though I do not reject the others, particularly the first. For Paul's very first premise is impossible—"if I speak with the tongues of angels." To speak with an angelic tongue is impossible for human beings, and he clearly emphasizes this impossibility by making distinction between the tongues of men and those of angels. There is no angelic tongue; while angels may speak to us in a human tongue men can never speak in those of angels.

As we are to understand the first clause—"If I speak with the tongues of angels"—as meaning, Were it as possible as it is impossible for me to speak with the tongues of angels; so are we to understand the second clause—"If I have all faith, so as to remove mountains"—to mean, Were it as possible as it is impossible to have such faith. Equally impossible is the proposition of understanding all mysteries, and we must take it to mean, Were it possible for one to understand all mysteries, which, however, it is not. John, in the last chapter of his Gospel, asserts that the world could not contain all the books which might be written concerning the things of the kingdom. For no man can ever fathom the depths of these mysteries. Paul's manner of expressing himself is but a very common one, such as: "Even if I were a Christian, if I believed not in Christ I would be nothing"; or, "Were you even a prince, if you neither ruled men nor possessed property you would be nothing."

And If I Bestow All My Goods to Feed the Poor

In other words, "Were I to perform all the good works on earth and yet had not charity—having sought therein only my own honor and profit and not my neighbor's—I would be lost." In the performance of external works so great as the surrender of property and life, Paul includes all works possible of performance, for he who would at all do these, would do any work. Just so, when he has reference to tongues he includes all good words and doctrines; and in prophecy, understanding and faith he comprises all wisdom and knowledge. Some may risk body and property for the sake of temporal glory. So Romans and pagans have done; but as love was lacking and they sought only their own interests, they practically gave nothing. It being generally impossible for men to give away all their property, and their bodies to be burned, the meaning must be: "Were it possible for me to give all my goods to the poor, and my body to be burned."

The false reasoning of the sophists will not stand when they maliciously deduct from this text the theory that the Christian faith is not effectual to blot out sin and to justify. They say that before faith can justify it must be garnished with love; but justification and its distinctive qualities as well are beyond their ken. Justification of necessity precedes love. One does not love until he has become godly and righteous. Love does not make us godly, but when one has become godly love is the result. Faith, the Spirit and justification have love as effect and fruitage, and not the mere ornament and supplement. We maintain that faith alone justifies and saves. But that we may not deceive ourselves and put our trust in a false faith, God requires love from us as the evidence of our faith, so that we may be sure of our faith being real faith.

The Nature of Christian Love

Love suffereth long, and is kind.

Now Paul begins to mention the nature of love, enabling us to perceive where real love and faith are to be found. A haughty teacher does not possess the virtues the apostle enumerates. Lacking these, however many gifts the haughty have received through the Gospel, they are devoid of love.

First, love "suffereth long." That is, it is patient; not sudden and swift to anger, not hasty to exercise revenge, impatience or blind rage. Rather it bears in patience with the wicked and the infirm until they yield. Haughty teachers can only judge, condemn and despise others, while justifying and exalting themselves.

Second, love is "kind." In other words, it is pleasant to deal with; is not of forbidding aspect; ignores no one; is kind to all men, in words, acts and attitude.

Third, love "envieth not"—is not envious nor displeased at the greater prosperity of others; grudges no one property or honor. Haughty teachers, however, are envious and unkind. They begrudge everyone else both honor and possessions. Though with their lips they may pretend otherwise, these characteristics are plainly visible in their deeds.

Fourth, love "vaunteth not itself." It is averse to knavery, to crafty guile and double-dealing. Haughty and deceptive spirits cannot refrain from such conduct, but love deals honestly and uprightly and face to face.

Fifth, love is not "puffed up," as are false teachers, who swell themselves up like adders.

Sixth, love "doth not behave itself unseemly" after the manner of the passionate, impatient and obstinate, those who presume to be always in the right, who are opposed to all men and yield to none, and who insist on submission from every individual, otherwise they set the world on fire, bluster and fume, shriek and complain, and thirst for revenge. That is what such inflating pride and haughtiness of which we have just spoken lead to.

Seventh, love "seeketh not her own." She seeks not financial advancement; not honor, profit, ease; not the preservation of body and life. Rather, she risks all these. In her is no such thing as the Church of Christ nor true Christians.

Eighth, love "is not [easily] provoked" by wrong and ingratitude; it is meek. False teachers can tolerate nothing, they seek only their own advantage and honor, to the injury of others.

Ninth, love "taketh not account of [thinketh no] evil." It is not suspicious; it puts the best construction on everything and takes all in good faith. The haughty, however, are immeasurably suspicious; always solicitous not to be underrated, they put the worst construction on everything, as Joab construed Abner's deeds (2 Sam. 3:25). This is a shameful vice and they who are guilty of it are hard to handle.

Tenth, love "rejoiceth not in unrighteousness [iniquity]." The words admit of two interpretations: First, as having reference to the delight in his own evil doings. Solomon (Prov. 2:14) speaks of those who "rejoice to do evil." Such must be either extremely profligate and shameless, characters like harlots and knaves; or else they must be hypocrites, who do not appreciate the wickedness of their conduct; characters like heretics and schismatics, who rejoice when their knavery succeeds under the name of God and of the truth. I do not accept this interpretation, but the other. Paul's meaning is that false teachers are malicious enough to prefer to hear, above all things, that some other does wrong, commits error and is brought to shame; and their motive is simply that they themselves may appear upright and godly. Such was the attitude of the pharisee toward the publican, in the Gospel. But love's compassion reaches far beyond its own sins, and prays for others.

Eleventh, love "rejoiceth with [in] the truth." Here is evidence that the preceding phrase is to be taken as having reference to malicious rejoicing at another's sin and fall. Rejoicing in the truth is simply exulting in the right-doing and integrity of another. Similarly, love is grieved at another's wrong-doing, but to the haughty it is an affliction to learn of uprightness in someone else; for they imagine such integrity detracts from their own profit and honor.

Twelfth, love "beareth all things." It excuses every failing in all men, however weak, unjust, or foolish one may be apparently, and no one can be guilty of a wrong too great for it to overlook. But none can do right in the eyes of the haughty, who ever find something to belittle and censure as beyond toleration.

Thirteenth, love "believeth all things." Paul does not here allude to faith in God, but to faith in men. His meaning is: Love is of decidedly trustful disposition. The possessor of it believes and trusts all men, considering them just and upright like himself. He anticipates no wily and crooked dealing, but permits himself to be deceived, deluded, flouted, imposed upon, at every man's pleasure, and asks, "Do you really believe men so wicked?" He measures all other hearts by his own, and makes mistakes with utmost cheerfulness. But such error works him no injury. He knows God cannot forsake, and the deceiver of love but deceives himself. The haughty, on the contrary, trust no one, will believe none, nor brook deception.

Fourteenth, love "hopeth all things." Love despairs of no man, however wicked he may be. It hopes for the best. As implied here, love says, "We must, indeed, hope for better things." It is plain from this that Paul is not alluding to hope in God. Love is a virtue particularly representing devotion to a neighbor; his welfare is its goal in thought and deed. Like its faith, the hope entertained by love is frequently misplaced, but it never gives up. Love rejects no man; it despairs of no cause. But the proud speedily despair of men generally, rejecting them as of no account.

Fifteenth, love "endureth all things." It endures whatever harm befalls, whatever injury it suffers; it endures when its faith and hope in men have been misplaced; endures when it sustains damage to body, property or honor. It knows that no harm has been done since it has a rich God. False teachers, however, bear with nothing, least of all with perfidy and the violation of plighted faith.

Sixteenth, love never faileth; that means, it abides forever, also in the life to come. It never gives up, never permits itself to be hindered or defeated by the wickedness or ingratitude of men, as do worldly individuals and false saints, who, immediately on perceiving contempt or ingratitude, draw back, unwilling to do further good to any, and rendering themselves quite inhuman, become perfect misanthropes like Timon in his reputation among the Greeks. Loves does not so. It permits not itself to be made wicked by the wickedness of men, nor to be hindered in well-doing. It continues to do good everywhere, teaching and admonishing, aiding and serving, notwithstanding its services and benefits must be rewarded, not by good, but by evil. Love remains constant and immovable; it continues, it endures, in this earthly life and also in the life to come. The apostle adds, "Whether there be prophecies, they shall be done away; whether there be tongues, they shall cease; whether there be knowledge, it shall be done away." Love he commends above all other endowments, as a gift that can never pass, even in the life to come. Those other gifts, the boast of the false apostles, are bestowed only for this present life, to serve in the administering of the ministerial office. Prophecy, tongues, knowledge, all must cease; for in yonder life each individual will himself perceive perfectly and there will be no need for one to teach another. Likewise, all differences, all inequalities, shall be no more. No knowledge and no diversity of gifts is necessary; God himself will be all in every soul (1 Cor. 15:28).

Here Paul gives utterance to the distinction between the life of faith here below and that heavenly life of divine vision. He would teach that we have in this life and the other the same possession, for it is the same God and the same treasures which we have here by faith and there by sight. In the objects themselves there is no difference; the difference consists in our knowledge. We have the same God in both lives, but in different manner of possession. The mode of possessing God in this life is faith. Faith is an imperfect, obscure vision, which makes necessary the Word, which, in turn, receives vogue through the ministry, tongues and prophecy. Without the Word, faith cannot live. But the mode of possessing God in the future life is not faith but sight. This is perfect knowledge, rendering unnecessary the Word, and likewise preaching, tongues and prophecy. These, then, must pass. Paul continues, "We know in part, and we prophesy in part."

"We know in part"; that is, in this life we know imperfectly, for it is of faith and not of sight. And we "prophesy in part";

that is, imperfectly, for the substance of our prophecy is the Word and preaching. Both knowledge and prophecy, however, reveal nothing short of what the angels see—the one God. "But when that which is perfect is come, that which is in part shall be done away."

He proves this by way of illustration and contrasts the child with the man. To children, who are yet weak, play is a necessity; it is a substitute for office and work. Similarly, we in the present life are far too frail to behold God. Until we are able, it is necessary that we should use the medium of Word and faith, which are adapted to our limitations. "For now we see in a mirror [through a glass] darkly; but then face to face."

Faith, Paul tells us, is like a mirror, like a riddle. The actual face is not in the glass; there is but the image of it. Likewise, faith gives us, not the radiant countenance of eternal Deity, but a mere image of him, an image derived through the Word. As a dark riddle points to something more than it expresses, so faith suggests something clearer than that which it perceives. But in the life to come, mirror and riddle, faith and its demonstration, shall all have ceased to be. God's face and our own shall be mutually and clearly revealed. Paul says, "Now I know in part; but then shall I know fully even as also I was fully known [know even also as I am known]." That is, God now knows me perfectly, clearly and plainly; no dark veil is upon myself. But as to him, a dark veil hides him from me. With the same perfect clearness wherewith he now knows me, I shall then know him—without a veil. The veil shall be taken away, not from him, but from me; for upon him is no veil.

The Greatest Christian Virtue Is Love

> But now abideth faith, hope, love, these three; and the greatest of these is love.

The sophists have transgressed in a masterly manner as regards this verse. They have made faith vastly inferior to love because of Paul's assertion that love is greater than faith and greater than hope. As usual, their mad reason blindly seizes upon the literal expression. They hack a piece out of it and the remainder they ignore. Thus they fail to understand Paul's meaning; they do not perceive that the sense of Paul concerning the greatness of love is expressed both in the text and the context. For surely it cannot be disputed that the apostle is here referring to the permanent or temporary character respectively of love and other gifts, and not to their rank or power. As to rank, not faith only, but the Word, surpasses love; for the Word is the power of God unto salvation to all that believe (Rom 1:16). Yet the Word must pass. But though love is the fruit of the Word and its effect, it shall never be abolished. Faith possesses God himself. It possesses and can accomplish all things; yet it must cease. Love gives and blesses the neighbor, as a result of faith, and it shall never be done away.

Now, Paul's statement that love is greater than faith and hope is intended as an expression of the permanence, or eternal duration, of love. Faith, being limited as to time in this temporary duration. With the same right I must say that the kingdom of Christ is greater upon earth than was Christ. Thereby I do not mean that the Church in itself is better and of higher rank than Christ, but merely that it covers a greater part of the earth than he compassed; for he was here but three years and those he spent in a limited sphere, whereas his kingdom has been from the beginning and is coextensive with the earth. In this sense, love I longer and broader than either faith or hope. Faith deals with God merely in the heart and in this life, whereas the relations of love both to God and the whole world are eternal. Nevertheless, as Christ is immeasurably better and higher and more previous than the Christian Church, although we behold him moving in smaller limits and as a mere individual, so is faith better, higher and more precious than love, though its duration is limited and it has God along for its object.

Paul's purpose in thus extolling love is to deal a blow to false teachers and to bring to naught their boasts about faith and other gifts when love is lacking. His thought is: "If ye possess not love, which abides forever, all else whereof ye boast being perishable, ye will perish with it. While the Word of God, and spiritual gifts, are eternal, yet the external office and proclamation of the Word, and likewise the employment of gifts in their variety, shall have an end, and thus your glory and pride shall become as ashes." So, then, faith justifies through the Word and produces love. But while both Word and faith shall pass, righteousness and love, which they effect, abide forever; just as a building erected by the aid of scaffolding remains after the scaffolding has been removed.

Observe how small the word "Love" and how easily uttered! Who would have thought to find so much precious virtue and power ascribed by Paul to this one excellence as counterpart of so much that is evil? This is, I imagine, magnifying love, painting love. It should justly shame the false teachers, who talk much of love but in whom not one of the virtues he mentions is found.

Every quality of love named by him means false teachers buffeted and assaulted. Whenever he magnifies love and characterizes her powers, he invariably makes at the same time a thrust at those who are deficient in any of them. Well may we, then, as he describes the several features, add the comment "But you do very differently."

It is passing strange that teachers devoid of love should possess such gifts as Paul has mentioned here, viz., speaking with tongues, prophesying, understanding mysteries; that they should have faith, should bestow their goods and suffer themselves to be burned. For we have seen what abominations ensue where love is lacking; such individuals are proud, envious, puffed up, impatient, unstable, false, venomous, suspicious, malicious, disdainful, bitter, disinclined to service, distrustful, selfish, ambitious and haughty. How can it consistently be claimed that people of this stamp can, through faith, remove mountains, give their bodies to be burned, prophesy, and so on? It is precisely as I have stated. Paul presents an impossible proposition, implying that since they are devoid of love, they do not really possess those gifts, but merely assume the name and appearance. And in order to divest them of those he admits for the sake of argument that they are what in reality they are not.

Preached at the Installation Service of the Rev. Dr. Gregory S. Cootsona

Carol Antablin Miles

I want to thank you, Greg, for entrusting me with the task of charging you as you begin your ministry here at the Fifth Avenue Presbyterian Church. As I sat down this week to think about what I might say to you, I was struck by how much of the same ground you and I have covered over the fourteen years that we've been friends. First we were students together at Berkeley, and then classmates at Princeton Seminary. We both followed the academic track and entered Ph.D. programs, and we both became first-time parents while working on our dissertations. We both did campus ministry at First Pres. Berkeley, and we both will have worked here at Fifth Avenue.

Over the years, you and I have had many of the same mentors, and pretty much the same core group of friends. We've even shared the same best friend, your wife, Laura. That's why I think it is especially courageous of you to have asked me to give you the charge this afternoon. I don't know how many men would invite their wife's closest friend to address them publicly on any subject of their choosing. Most would probably fear that some intimate details about their life would be exposed, or that someone like me might take the opportunity to talk about something really personal, like your marriage.

Well, that is exactly what I'm going to do today. I want to talk to you about your marriage, Greg. But not your marriage to Laura. I want to talk to you about your "marriage" to this church. Because if you think about it, that is essentially what we're here to recognize and celebrate this afternoon.

Having just gone through the search process, you no doubt heard people refer to the relationship between a pastor nominating committee and a candidate as a courtship. And I'm sure that you were advised by more experienced pastors to beware of the pitfalls of such a relationship. "Be careful," they say. "You get engaged to the committee, but you marry the whole congregation!"

But now, after weeks of getting to know each other over shared meals, through letters and cross-country phone calls, you and this congregation have chosen each other. You've sensed a certain chemistry between you, and now you hope it will lead to a good marriage.

That is why the text I've chosen to read as part of this charge is one that is often read at weddings. It's a hard text for us to listen to in any other context because we're so used to hearing it read by a friend of the bride or groom. But the truth is, this passage from 1 Corinthians 13 is much more appropriate for an occasion like your service of installation, because in it, as you know, Paul is speaking not of romantic love at all, but of church ministry! Let me read it for us from a recent translation by another Presbyterian minister, and see if we can give it a fresh hearing. Let us listen for the word of God to us:

> If I speak with human eloquence and angelic ecstasy but don't love, I'm nothing but the creaking of a rusty gate.
>
> If I speak God's Word with power, revealing all his mysteries and making everything plain as day, and if I have faith that says to a mountain, "Jump," and it jumps, but I don't love, I'm nothing.
>
> If I give everything I own to the poor and even go to the stake to be burned as a martyr, but I don't love, I've gotten nowhere. So, no matter what I say, what I believe, and what I do, I'm bankrupt without love.
>
> Love never gives up.
>
> Love cares more for others than for self.
>
> Love doesn't want what it doesn't have.
>
> Love doesn't strut.
>
> Doesn't have a swelled head,
>
> Doesn't force itself on others,
>
> Isn't always "me first,"

Doesn't fly off the handle,

Doesn't keep score of the sins of others,

Doesn't revel when others grovel,

Takes pleasure in the flowering of truth,

Puts up with anything,

Trusts God always,

Always looks for the best,

Never looks back,

But keeps going to the end.

Love never dies. Inspired speech will be over some day; praying in tongues will end; understanding will reach its limit. We know only a portion of the truth, and what we say about God is always incomplete. But when the Complete arrives, our incompletes will be canceled.

When I was an infant at my mother's breast, I gurgled and cooed like any infant. When I grew up, I left those infant ways for good.

We don't yet see things clearly. We're squinting in a fog, peering through a mist. But it won't be long before the weather clears and the sun shines bright! We'll see it all then, see it all as clearly as God sees us, knowing him directly just as he knows us!

But for right now, until that completeness, we have three things to do to lead us toward that consummation: Trust steadily in God, hope unswervingly, love extravagantly, And the best of the three is love. (THE MESSAGE)

What is the connection between romantic love and pastoral ministry? Why is marriage such an apt metaphor for your work with the congregation here at Fifth Avenue Church? Perhaps it's because in a very real sense the two of you have entered into a covenant relationship with each other. You even took vows a few moments ago to affirm your commitment to each other. But there is more to it than that.

You probably have heard those same experienced pastors speak of a new minister's first weeks and months with a congregation as a "honeymoon" period. But we all know that while the honeymoon can be sweet and dizzying and loaded with romance, the true heart of any marriage lies in the day-to-day living of life together. It's the deepening of regard for each other that comes about through the shared experience of shopping for food, doing the laundry, caring for children or pets, decorating the apartment, scheduling dentist appointments, and visits to your in-laws. And we all know that there is nothing romantic about any of that.

Greg, it is quite possible that you may have a wonderfully romantic honeymoon with the Fifth Avenue Presbyterian Church. I hope you do. My husband and I found it easy to fall in love with the members of this congregation and with New York City itself. You will be continually amazed and impressed by the quality of people you will come to know here. It can be dizzying. And you will be called upon to do things in your ministry that will be thrilling for you, teaching and preaching and sharing ideas with some of the sharpest and most creative people in the country.

But I feel I must tell you now that you may be surprised by how much of your ministry here will consist of the mundane things of church life. You may be amazed by how much time you will spend writing copy for the church newsletter or designing a new brochure for the Christian Education Commission. And it may not be in speaking at one of the Wednesday night dinners, but in serving at one of the Wednesday night dinners because there were not enough volunteers that night, that you will experience the heart of your ministry within this church.

When the romance is over, it is love that abides.

Just as there is nothing particularly romantic about the day in, day out work of ministry, there is nothing theoretical about it either. I remember when I was single, I used to have a mental list of qualities I was looking for in a potential mate. And I suppose there was some benefit to such an exercise of the imagination. But on the other side of marriage, I can say with confidence that no such person exists or will ever exist who can live up to what we have theorized to be the perfect husband or wife. We never marry a list of qualities, we marry a particular person, with his or her own unique character and style and background and way of being in the world. And discovering this person in all of his or her uniqueness is where the richness lies.

Now I'm very aware of the temptation faced by people like you and me, Greg, academics who have spent the better part of our lives holed up in scholarly communities doing nothing but learning and generating theories. It would be easy for us to forget that there is absolutely nothing theoretical about our work in the parish. And it can come as quite a shock to those of us arriving from the academy to discover that the church we now serve looks nothing like the churches described in the book of Acts, or Calvin's Geneva, or the Presbyterian Book of Order. We always serve a particular congregation, with its own unique character and qualities, history and style. And we must embrace that truth. Because parish ministry is not about trying to make a congregation fit our ideal picture of the church, or turn them into a church that does and believes everything just right. Parish ministry is about discovering the depth of a congregation, loving it with all its quirks and idiosyncrasies, and then respecting and cultivating what we discern God to already be doing in their midst. That is where the richness lies.

Where our theological sophistication and theories fail us, love abides.

But these are truths we often discover only with time. As is this one final truth. So often in a relationship with a spouse or a potential spouse we start out looking for ways this person can enhance our lives. While we are still dating, and sometimes well into the marriage, we find ourselves scrutinizing our partners and evaluating them for what they can give or do or be for us.

And it is only with time that we discover that true ministry is not interested in what a congregation can give or do or be for us. True ministry is interested in how we can help a church and its members become all that God has created and desires them to be. How we can love them with the same love Christ has for the church, a love that never gives up, cares more for others than for self, doesn't want what it doesn't have, doesn't keep score, always looks for the best, keeps on going to the end. That is why God has given us, pastors and congregations, to each other as a gift.

And you are certainly a gift to this church, Greg. You have so much to offer this congregation, and it has much to offer you. You come with energy, intelligence, imagination, and a whole host of other talents and abilities. But of all the gifts you may have to bring to the people of the Fifth Avenue Presbyterian Church, the greatest of them is love.

Love Story

Beth Ann Miller

I don't always find it easy to visit the nursing home. Some days I can go more readily than others. I'm sure part of the reason is that my own youth and vitality, my sense of life being open and unlimited, all that comes up against the facts—I am mortal; my life is limited, and my body will not forever move with ease. Someday, I too may be one who forgets who she is, where she is. I too may one day be confined to bed, totally dependent on the care of others. I too may sit in my chair, imprisoned by my physical body, waiting for a friendly voice, a familiar face. I too may have to wait for those caught up in their busy, busy worlds to take time out to remember me. It's much easier to pretend that this part of living isn't happening, especially for those of us who are at the beginning or peaks of our careers, or those of us raising children, or planning the next vacation.

Some days, it's hard to go visit, and going always evokes questions in me: Is this necessary, God? Does it have to be this way? Can't your mercy extend a little further? I don't have the answers yet; I'm sure I never will.

There's one friend I've been going to see for six years now. I no longer ask what she wants me to read to her from scripture. It's always the same, and in this case, her memory is better than mine. On my last visit I forgot to take my Bible and I couldn't locate hers. But, no matter, she began to say it by heart: "If I speak in the tongues of men and of angels, but have not love...love is patient and kind...love never ends." Maybe it is the only thing that can transcend the pain of arthritic joints, a failing mind, and despair. Indeed, it is love that finally, ultimately keeps any of us from sitting down and giving up or going crazy...but not cheap love, not easy love.

There's plenty of that around. It's the kind proclaimed on bumper stickers: I love New York; I love my golden retriever; I love Carolina; or I love Duke. Romantic songs that equate love with lust pulsate from the radio or MTV. The problem is that romance isn't forever. When the stars and tingling feelings fade, the conclusion is: "We don't love each other anymore. Call the attorney."

If the only love we've known is the love that says, "I love you for better, but not worse; I'll take you on your good days, but not on the bad ones," we have not been loved very well. And if we can only love people when they meet our expectations and fulfill our needs, we do not yet understand what it means to love.

Often, when we hear 1 Corinthians 13 read, we listen halfheartedly and smile and nod at the words. They are very poetic and beautiful, but if we listen with full attention, we realize there is nothing easy about the love of which Paul speaks. He directs his words to the Corinthian church. After all, the church is the one place, above all others, where we expect to find love, but even here it can be disguised as something it is not.

When the Corinthians inquired about spiritual gifts, they weren't expecting to hear all this stuff about love...what did that have to do with measuring your religious status? You can see when someone has the gifts of tongues, prophecy, miracles, healing, teaching, administration. Aren't those things enough to entice others into the church?

There's for example, John over there. Some think he's just a young upstart who has a lot of idealistic opinions. But he is serious about prophesying. He sure can stir up a crowd. After all, any prophet worth his or her salt will make others angry. You have to comfort the afflicted but afflict the comfortable.

Over there is Elizabeth, who has been given the ability to speak in tongues, and it has enriched her spiritual life. She just wishes that her neighbor Anna had the same gift. Anna just needs to open her life more to the Lord and immerse herself in the Word.

And James—he is renowned for the way he teaches the men's Torah class. He's been teaching it for fifty years now. But he got pretty offended recently when someone suggested he might want to retire and let one of the younger men teach.

Susannah is known for her deep faith, and she prays that others might be as strong as she is. When tough times come, she tells others, "Keep your chin up. Trust the Lord. There's a reason for this."

They must have been surprised when Paul stated, "And I will show you a still more excellent way," and then launched into an attack on religious values. Prophetic powers, knowledge, faith, giving your body to be burned—these things mean nothing if not motivated by love.

We don't hear of too many people being martyred anymore, and the only prophesying we hear about is the street-corner preacher who shouts at us to repent or burn. But there are other religious experiences that are valued and admired.

I remember, while in college, attending a campus ministry group before I decided to became an affiliate member of the Presbyterian church in town. That church was a place I found nurturing, and I heard the good news in a way I had not heard it before. I attended a Bible study there led by a minister, Rev. Foster, who was very gentle and kind and surprisingly open to the reflections of college students. One day I ran into an acquaintance I had met in the campus ministry group. When I told her about my new affiliation with the Presbyterian church, she looked at me with sympathy and skepticism and said, "Well, I hope you'll get what you need there to grow." My experience wasn't hers, so she questioned the validity of my faith journey. Needless to say, I felt judged.

Moral heroism is another religious quality much admired today. I'm all for morality. Heaven knows, the world needs more of it. But sometimes that too becomes a way for folks to pride themselves on righteousness. Who can fault someone with impeccable morals? They must walk closer to God. But few of us can stand in the light of their judgment either.

Those who value personal piety and goodness above all else are as noisy gongs or clanging cymbals. You can never really get close to them, and you won't hear, in all their religious talk, anything that makes you want to be part of the kingdom. But have someone show you their willingness to share the story of your life—well, that's another message altogether. Especially if they're willing to hang around for the sorrow as well as the joy, the despair as well as the hope, the anger as well as the laughter, the doubt as well as the faith, the failure as well as the success. What we really need and want is someone to love the saint and the sinner, the wise person and the fool that are inside all of us. That kind of love is hard to resist.

C. S. Lewis observed that our human loving is "mostly a craving to be loved." And let's face it, that is true! That is why we are here today, I do believe. We are each seeking and responding to that Love Divine, all loves excelling, which continues to be patient with us. Indeed this Love is the One that cries out, a broken heart notwithstanding, "How can I give you up? I am God, the Holy One." That kind of love is more than a feeling; it is totally self-giving.

When I was in high school, the movie *Love Story* hit the theaters. I watched it and wept like most other teenagers. And probably, at the time, I thought its most famous line was wonderful: "Love means never having to say you're sorry." Thank goodness I've matured in my understanding of love. For love that excuses all wrong as inconsequential, love that doesn't admit hurt, is not real love. It can never really forgive or heal or comfort.

Jesus, during his ministry, told a number of love stories. He told one about a prodigal son. The point wasn't that you can get away with murder and still come home. He told it to let us know about a parent who thought he'd lost his child forever, but waited, hoping against hope, for his return. And when he heard the car turn into the drive and knew his child was safe, he ran to hug his neck and celebrate. Have you ever had your life given back to you after you had squandered it some way, somehow? Don't think it didn't cost others or God some pain. But sometimes love endures it all, and you are given another chance.

Jesus talked about a shepherd who had a hundred sheep, but one strayed away. So the shepherd went looking for it. There may be a thousand people on the church roll, but the shepherd is out there looking for the one who needs to be part of "the tie that binds our hearts in Christian love." Love hopes all things for us, so searches us out.

Jesus told many more stories, but a common thread was a relentless love. Then he stopped telling the story; he acted it out. And that is the most complete expression of love. Jesus did not stand on Calvary and announce, "I feel for all of you." He died on a cross, where love and sorrow flowed mingling down. The greatest love story ends with a beginning–love that triumphs over evil and death.

I've pondered hard this week this love that doesn't end. I had a hard time thinking about the power of it and how to illustrate it. I'm sure it had to do with my dad's surgery. As so many of you know, anytime you hear the word *cancer,* you begin to think the worst. You want to know how much time do you have left with the one you love? Maybe, deep down, I have been most afraid that if he died, so too would his love be taken away from me. But now I see Dad's illness has given this love a new context. His love is forever a part of me. And I knew I loved him, but now I know how much...and I realize that love won't quit.

You who have lost someone close to you understand that. The widow visits the cemetery every week and puts fresh flowers on the grave. The family sits and tells "remember whens" about a parent or child who has died. Love never ends.

There are times it seems it should end. There are marriages that suffer because of infidelity. You have a full right to stop loving, even a biblical right to divorce, but you don't. Who can explain the feelings and betrayal? But sometimes it happens. Love does not end.

Your kids get into the wrong crowd and they begin to make bad choices and mess up their lives. They do things that make you distrust them. They may lie to you and reject your help.

But your heart keeps breaking for them, keeps hoping for them. Love doesn't end.

This week, serial killer Ted Bundy was executed, and the people lined up outside the prison and cheered when they were told he was dead. His mother said, "He'll always be my precious son." Who can explain that? Love doesn't end.

In the nursing home, my friend waits. She knows she won't ever be young again, or out of bed and moving around again, and yet is comforted because love never ends.

It is a mystery, this Love, because it does triumph over sin and suffering and death. And whenever it is enacted in our relationships with one another, then we have been empowered by a Love beyond ourselves. Of all the powers this world knows, this is the one that cannot be coerced or wielded or achieved. It is a gift. It is the greatest spiritual gift. And in that love, we live and move and have our being, now and forever. Thanks be to God!

Love: God's Greatest Gift

Gary B. Nelson

Listen again to the words of Saint Paul:

> I may speak in tongues of men or of angels, but if I have no love, I am a sounding gong or a clanging cymbal. I may have the gift of prophecy and the knowledge of every hidden truth; I may have faith enough to move mountains; but if I have no love, I am nothing. I may give all I possess to the needy, I may give my body to be burnt, but if I have no love, I gain nothing by it.
>
> Love is patient and kind. Love envies no one, is never boastful, never conceited, never rude; love is never selfish, never quick to take offence. Love keeps no score of wrongs, takes no pleasure in the sins of others, but delights in the truth. There is nothing love cannot face; there is no limit to its faith, its hope, its endurance.
>
> Love will never come to an end. Prophecies will cease; tongues of ecstasy will fall silent; knowledge will vanish. For our knowledge and our prophecy alike are partial,

and the partial vanishes when wholeness comes. When I was a child I spoke like a child, thought like a child, reasoned like a child; but when I grew up I finished with childish things. At present we see only puzzling reflections in a mirror, but one day we shall see face to face. My knowledge now is partial; then it will be whole, like God's knowledge of me. There are three things that last for ever: faith, hope, and love; and the greatest of the three is love. (REB)

I can't tell you how many books I've read, how many songs I've listened to, or how many sermons I've heard on this text; yet I sometimes wonder if anyone knows what these words really mean. Almost one out of two people I marry will end up in divorce; teen pregnancy is rising at an alarming rate; talk shows are filled with people who are just plain unhappy and unfulfilled. While I speak, another spouse is being abused, and before this sermon ends, another child will die from either abuse or neglect.

Yes, sometimes I wonder if anyone knows what love really is. Saint Paul wondered too. He was engaged in a heavy discussion with the church at Corinth. It was like a bad marriage. The people were bickering and fighting, arguing about who had the greatest of the spiritual gifts. The physicians were claiming that healing was the best of the gifts. Some were claiming that miracles were the proof that they were superior, and others claimed that speaking in tongues was the true sign of the way to God.

To address all this Paul says to them, "Here, I will show you an even better way." If seeking happiness or fulfillment, if seeking better gifts, one thing is necessary: Love must be the mainspring and the guiding force. The "better way" Paul refers to may be the better way to gain the greater gifts, or it may mean that Paul will now tell the Corinthians about something else that is more important than any gift, namely love. Not the sentimental, romantic kind of love, but Christian love.

Chapter 13 is Paul's great hymn of Christian love. He exalts love as the supreme gift, not only in what it is and what it does, or itself, but also in what it contributes to other gifts.

The Greek word Paul uses for love is *agape,* the same word he used to identify the "love feast" back in chapter 11. It designates the highest kind of love, far removed from the sex-love and passion that saturate our culture.

It is also higher than affection or personal liking or the attachment of friends. It is love like God's love for the world in John 3:16. God loved this fallen world filled with hate, abuse, greed, and rebellion. We were really unworthy of any kind of divine love, but God chose to love us anyway, never giving up on us. Although God clearly saw all our weaknesses and sinfulness, he devoted himself to our welfare so deeply and intensely that he made the supreme sacrifice for our sin; God gave his one and only Son to save a fallen world. Such love is more than fondness and affection. It is the highest kind of love. It seeks the welfare of those who are utterly unworthy of any kindness and concern.

We chuckle at city-bred children who believe that eggs come from cartons and milk from plastic jugs, confusing the container with the source. But there are adults who are just as confused about love, foolishly believing that love originates in the human heart. But love always comes from God. God takes the initiative, and we are merely the containers. Better yet, we are the pipelines and channels for that love. The Spirit pours God's love into our lives, and we irrigate the world by sharing that love. The more we give away, the more we receive. And the more we refuse to love others, the more we shut ourselves off from God's love.

So our love is to reflect this divine love. In our love for our fellow human beings we are also to rise above our sentimentality and emotions, and devote ourselves to their welfare, even if there is nothing lovable about them, even if they repel us and their conduct outrages us or disgusts us. First Corinthians 13 says that this is the way of real love.

Without this love, this *agape,* even the greatest gifts and noblest deeds have no value. The Corinthians were inordinately proud of their gift of speaking in tongues. It was a gift they sought after and loved to display. But even if they could have spoken in the tongues of angels, their feat would have been no more than an impressive display of sound and noise, if they used this gift without Christian love.

Even if they could prophesy like Jeremiah and preach like Peter at Pentecost; even if they could "fathom" more mysteries and knowledge than God permitted Paul to do; even if they had "faith that can move mountains," these glorious achievements would be worthless if agape were not motivating them. For all their great feats, they would be nothing.

Supreme sacrifices are also nothing if Christian love does not inspire us. In one grand sweep we could turn over everything we own to charity; in one splendid sacrifice we could give our lives in fiery martyrdom for a noble cause, but if such sacrifice were brought without Christian love, we would be nothing.

Such is love's supreme value for the greatest gifts and achievements of believers. Such love is worthy of some of the most poetic and most exalted words the inspired apostle ever wrote.

Paul then goes on to present Christian love in a personal way. Love is patient–longsuffering, as the King James Version has it. Love is kind. Kindness here is not so much a sweet disposition as it is the practice of useful, beneficial, friendly acts. Love is not jealous, it doesn't brag, it doesn't put on airs. It doesn't have "inflated ideas of its own importance," as one translation puts it.

Love isn't rude or ill-mannered. Good manners are more than etiquette; they are ways of showing respect for the feelings of others. Love is not self-seeking. Love always seeks the welfare of others. It is not easily angered–touchy, as one translation puts it. It doesn't flare up every time our pride is hurt. Love keeps no record of wrongs. It doesn't keep score of all the bad things others say about us or do to us–to make sure they will be repaid in full.

Love does not delight in evil. It isn't glad when evil or injustice is done. Instead, it rejoices in the truth. Here *truth* and *righteousness* are the same. Love is not softness. It doesn't erase the boundary between right and wrong. Love always protects. It can overlook faults. First Peter says that "love covers over a multitude of sins."

The Greek word for *protects* may also be translated *bears* or *endures*. Love always trusts. It is not gullible but has faith. It is ready to believe the best about everyone. Love always hopes.

It is not pessimistic; it can count on God's grace. Paul hoped even in the case of the unbelieving Jews who hardened their hearts against the gospel. Finally, love always perseveres. It endures all the trials of life with fortitude. It does not lose heart.

Paul does not describe love in its greatest works, sacrifices, martyrdoms, triumphs; instead he goes into the ordinary circumstances of life as we meet them day by day and shows us the picture of love as it must be under these.

When Paul writes "love never fails," he declares that love is greater than other gifts and qualities. It endures; all else passes away. Prophecies will cease. Whether they are miraculous, foretelling future events, or whether they include preaching and teaching today, the day will come when they will no longer be needed. Speaking in tongues as the gift existed in the first century has ceased. There will also be a day when the exercise of spiritual knowledge as we know it will come to an end.

Our spiritual knowledge and our prophetic proclamation of God's word are not complete even today. We know in part and we prophesy in part. Paul says that it's like seeing an image in a poor-looking glass or mirror, compared with seeing the actual object directly and clearly. There are many things in scripture that are not as clear to us today as they will be at the end times. They are still clear enough for us in this life, however, to see our way to our heavenly home, where we shall know fully and see clearly as God now knows us.

Christian love, agape, abides to all eternity. So will faith and hope, but this love is greater than either of these. In heaven there will still be hope. Even though we shall have attained the goal of our hope, eternal life, yet we shall hope for ever new joys to experience in heaven.

Why is Christian love greater than either faith or hope? Paul does not tell us. Perhaps the best answer is that of Johann Bengel, who said: "God is not called faith or hope directly, he is called love." God does not simply give love, God *is* love.

We may also say that love brings us into the fullest union and communion with God and that love is God's greatest gift. But even if we cannot grasp all of Paul's meaning, we dare never forget that love is the greatest of all our gifts and qualities. Without that love we cannot understand God or what it means to be a Christian.

"Faith, hope, and love abide," Paul tells the Corinthians. These are the certainties that will see us safely through life. But in the age to come, faith will be replaced with certainty. Hope will give way to fulfillment. In the kingdom of Christ only love will remain. Love never ends because only love can bridge this world and the world to come.

Amen.

Saints Cyril and Methodius, Valentine's Day, and True Love
Paul Rorem

Today, February 14, is a major "saints' day." No, not Saint Valentine, despite the lesson read about love. That's the legend of the early martyr(s) Valentinus. That minor saint's day has nothing to do with flowers, chocolate, or Hallmark cards, nothing even to do with love. The whole phenomenon of "Valentine's Day" and love grew up around February 14 for other reasons to do with spring and mating. No, the major saints' day today is the commemoration of Saints Cyril and Methodius, brothers, missionaries, scholars, patrons of ecumenism and of cross-cultural communication.

Apostles of Christ to the Slavic peoples, Cyril and Methodius were missionaries in the ninth century, the age of Christendom. When we imply that Christendom, from Constantine's conversion to our own time, never took seriously the challenges of evangelism or mission, we miss the chance to learn something for our own task, especially from examples such as that of Cyril and Methodius. For one thing, Cyril and Methodius represented ecumenical cooperation in mission—sent by the Greek church, then fully cooperative with Rome, and eventually honored by Rome.

In presenting Christ to Moravia, Slovakia, Croatia, and Serbia, Cyril and Methodius remain one of the few points of agreement even between Czechs and Slovaks, Roman Catholic Croatians and Orthodox Serbs in times of strife and warfare.

Further, beyond ecumenical witness, Cyril and Methodius pioneered cross-cultural communication in mission. Some people back then thought that the only appropriate church languages were the three on the cross—Hebrew, Greek, and Latin—which would leave most of us in big trouble! Cyril and Methodius insisted on translations of the Bible and the liturgy into the vernacular, the common language of the Slovak peoples. Methodius, especially, championed a liturgy in the language of the people. Cyril worked so hard on developing a written form for the local language that he is credited with the development of "Old Church Slavonic" and even the name of the script "Cyrillic," for modern Russian.

We can learn from such ecumenical and cross-cultural pioneers, on the saints' day that commemorates them. But now, what have Cyril and Methodius to do with 1 Corinthians 13 and Valentine's Day? In general, we can learn the message of the scriptures from such saints, even something new about an old standby, this well-known description of love.

The famous "love chapter" is most popular at weddings. Non-Christians must think it our main creed! In that context, it starts to sound like romantic idealism. For some reality therapy, try to put in the names of groom and bride.

Love is patient and kind, for example. Can we say, "The groom is patient and kind"? An old married couple once said, "One of us is always patient and kind." Which one? "We take turns," they said.

It almost works, to put human names in. But how far can we get in the text?

"Paul," for example, is not jealous or boastful, arrogant or rude? "Kate" does not insist on her own way, is never irritable or resentful? No one can honestly put one's own name in as *the* example of such love, or even the name of one's beloved, at least not when it comes to such perfection: "Love bears all things"; "Love never ends." For our loves and our lives have their limits.

But "God *is* love." And if we substitute God's name, it works. God is patient. God is kind. God is not envious or boastful or arrogant or rude. God does not rejoice at wrong but rejoices in the right.

As for ourselves, the paradigm of this perfect love shows our frailties, the weakness of our loves and our lives. Only perfect love, God as love, seems to qualify, and yet that seems so far away.

So we look for examples closer to home. Perhaps the great saints of the church? Does *that* work? Cyril and Methodius, for example. Cyril is never irritable? Methodius never arrogant or rude?

In fact, Cyril *was* sometimes hard to take; Methodius insisted on *his* own way often enough. He was brought up on charges of heterodoxy and disobedience! *But* they trusted finally not in themselves, but in another. None of the saints, not even their original predecessors, the apostles themselves, can stand up to the test of this chapter. Bickering, wavering, asleep at the time of trial, even the apostles could not claim to embody such love. Not even they "endured all things." Against this standard, "none is righteous; no, not one."

Well, there *was* one, patient with crowds, kind with children and disciples alike. There was one who was never envious or boastful, arrogant or rude, never irritable or resentful.

The apostles, Cyril and Methodius, and all the missionaries and saints of the church knew where to find love–perfect love and down-to-earth love, love incarnate, all loves excelling.

"By this, we know love, that he laid down his life for us."

He it was who bore all things, endured all things, even death, and yet who "never ends."

The center of God's love is Christ, who therefore sets the standard for this famous passage on love. It is Christ, God's love incarnate, who bears all things, and endures all things, and who never ends. Left to our own performance, we brides and grooms, all human valentines, and even the kindly hearts among us all fail to measure up to such perfection.

But with Christ as God's perfect love for us fulfilling the demands of perfect love, we are free to enjoy what loves and lives we have, short of absolute perfection.

Once we remember the true definition of love and keep first things first, then we can also appreciate the saints, frail and human as they were—Cyril, Methodius, even the legendary Saint Valentine and this curious tradition of Valentine's Day.

The More Excellent Way

Clayton J. Schmit

Of the many choices we have to make in life, many are small and inconsequential: What shall I have for dinner? What kind of clothes shall I put on? What flavor ice cream should I choose? Other choices are more important, monumental, and momentous. What will I be when I grow up? Where will I go to college or trade school? Should I get married? Should I have children? Where will I retire?

One great decision all people face is this: What kind of person will I be? How do I choose to be in the world? Will I be gentle and kind, loving and life-giving? Or will I be rough, crude, and profane? Will I hide who I am behind a front of glamour or bravado, or will I be open and vulnerable? Will I be soft-spoken and friendly, or gruff and disagreeable? I know two people who made rather odd choices in this regard. Oddly, they are both pastors. He and she are both fond of conflict. Each, in his and her own way, likes to find ways to keep things stirred up around them. They tend to choose not the kindest ways to say things to people. It is no surprise that their churches have been filled with conflict.

What kind of person will I be? The answer, we might hope, is that it is simply a matter of being ourselves. A New York billboard asks the question: "Why be yourself when you can be someone else?" For those who cannot figure out how to be themselves, or don't want to be, there are many who want to help them choose who they can be. There are self-help gurus who are famous for working with movie stars and pop musicians. There are pseudo-religious writers who put a New Age spin on traditional moral standards. There are the people who write advertisements for the army, telling you to "Be all you can be," as if toting a gun and being trained to kill were the fulfillment of God's greatest hope for your life. There are radio and television talk-show hosts who barrage you with one-sided preachments about being on the left or the right. And there are fitness infomercials that try to convince you that being lean and muscle-bound is the real you and that using their equipment is the way to become most fully yourself.

There are many ways to be in the world. With all this input, it can be easy to make some poor choices. Occasionally, we all make some bad choices, choosing to follow paths that lead us nowhere, into unproductive dead ends. Or we may choose paths that lead us to conflict and disharmony, like those two pastors who led their churches into dissension and division.

The church of Corinth was filled with dissension. Saint Paul had a stake in the church he had founded in that city. Hearing of their arguments and division, Paul penned this letter that we know as First Corinthians. Specifically, their problem was that members of the church had chosen to fight with one another over their way of being the community of Christ. They were fighting over who was the most important in the church. God had blessed them with many spiritual gifts. Some had the gift to preach, some to prophesy, some to teach, some to heal, some to lead, and some to speak in tongues. All of these gifts, as manifestations of the Holy Spirit, should have given rise to the church's smooth operation. Instead, they led to constant bickering over whose role was most important.

Into the midst of this fire of discontent, Paul pours these cooling words from our text. They begin with this: "I will show you a still more excellent way." Lay down your arguments, Paul says. Set aside any thought of who is best or who is right. Do not begrudge your neighbors' use of the gifts the Spirit brings. Love is a choice, after all. You can act as you will. To be disagreeable, to foster disharmony, to fight over what God has given you. Or you can choose to be patient and kind, humble and gracious, life-giving and forgiving. You can choose to guard your lips and discipline your actions. To act in love is, Paul teaches, an important choice.

But it also much more than a choice. The most excellent part is that love is principally a gift. Not a rule that must be followed, though such a rule would benefit the world if it could be legislated. Not an example to emulate, though both Jesus and Paul lived lives worthy to model. Not a formula to be followed, though simple kindness would ease tense moments anywhere. But the way of love is not a law, a model, or a gimmick. It is a gift. A spiritual gift. A gift of the Spirit, given to the church to shape its many parts into the unity of a single body. All gifts are important, but only one is critical to the church's unity, and only one can be shared by all in the community. It is the gift of love, springing from the fountainhead of God's good pleasure, flowing from the wounds of Christ, whose death unlocked a reservoir of unbounded charity. To swim in the flow of this limitless stream is to live in love. A choice, yes, but also a current that compels us to be the church in unity and faith. For the power of love to guide and unite us, let us pray:

Gracious God, Giver of all good things, we thank you for these timeless teachings of Paul, who saw so clearly what our vision dims. We thank you for your Son, Jesus, who lived the life of love and demonstrated its simple power. Above all, we thank you for this sacrifice that loosed anew your love into the world. Teach us to love in all we do. Of all that you give us, let this spiritual gift be ours in fullest measure. Let it bind us together as your people, one body in which we take joy and delight in one another's diversity and complexity. Let this gift be ours, O God, for the sake of him who first loved us, Jesus Christ our Lord.

Amen.

1 Corinthians 13:1–13

Kathy Singh

I always enjoy hearing this famous love passage. Many of us know it so well. It sounds like music to our ears.

Love, love–our society is driven by talk of love: love between a woman and a man, love between parents and child, love of one's animals, love of country, job, money, car, home. Always when we hear of love, it is in relationship to someone or something. Love cannot be out of relationship. Even if you are in love with yourself, it is in relationship.

Love in relationship is exactly what Paul is talking about in this lesson for today. But his view, and indeed the Christian view of love, is not the world's view of love. Paul begins this passage by telling us that even if we can speak in the language of angels, or have the gift of prophecy, or know all mysteries, or even have so much faith as to remove mountains, but do not have love, we are nothing.

What? I thought that these were great gifts from God. How can they be nothing if they are from God? Didn't Paul in chapter 12 tell us that there are varieties of gifts, but the same Spirit, varieties of service, but the same Lord, that the same God activates them all? If they are from God, how can he now say that they are nothing?

Let's look more carefully at what he is saying. In each case, his qualifier for the value of the gift given is love. For the gift to be of value, it must be connected with love. Why is this so important? Why isn't it enough that these gifts are God-given?

We learn why when we look at the Corinthian congregation. This early Christian community is a troubled group. So troubled that Paul had to write them several letters. As we read this letter, we see that there are divisions among them. They have been quarreling over which leader to follow. They have been tolerating the blatant immoral behavior of a few of their members. Some of these Christians have been eating the food sacrificed to idols. Most offensive of all is that when they have come together for the Lord's supper, they have been callous and have partaken of the meal without waiting for the slave and blue-collar Christians to get there.

Yet the people in this community have been gifted spiritually. They can speak in tongues, some can prophesy, but they are misusing these gifts. They are using them to parade their importance before others within the congregation–a kind of "one-upmanship" because they have been blessed and gifted. They are puffing themselves up because of these gifts. Thus, the gift that was meant to glorify God, to build up the body of Christ–the church–is being used to glorify the individual, to build up the individual. The result of this self-glorification is division within the church.

Now, how does this apply today? You say we Lutherans don't speak in tongues or prophesy. So, of course, this doesn't apply to us. But what do we parade before others? What do we puff ourselves up over? Are we puffed up over how prestigious our jobs are? how much money we make? how much education we have? how big our houses are? Or here, in this church community, how long we've been a member? how important we think our opinion is about how things ought to be done?

Does our puffed-up status lead us to be less considerate of some within this community: those who are less educated, those who have fewer financial resources, those who are younger, those who are elderly? Do we think our opinion about how we ought to worship and how to lead the church is more valuable than any of these who were just mentioned?

Paul says this makes us a clashing cymbal. Even if we do other good works, even if we give away all our possessions, without love this makes us nothing. A gong!

Wait a minute here, if love is not giving away all your possessions, then what is love?

For Paul, the origin of love is not human love. It is the love of God, the love of God that has been shown in Christ. The self-giving love of Christ, the total self-emptying of Christ on the cross. Undeserved and unmerited love. Given, not because we were so good or worshipful, but as Paul writes in Romans, Christ died for us not because we were good, but while we were yet sinners. Through this act on the cross and in the waters of our baptism, we are made new creatures, created through the love of God in Christ Jesus. This is the love of which Paul speaks.

Love not based on how deserving someone is or how important someone is, love…simply for being, for being a child of God. This is the lens through which baptized Christians are called to view others. This is being conformed to the image of Christ.

What does this image look like? Paul tells us. It looks like waiting patiently, like showing mercy and kindness, like humbling oneself, like behaving honorably, like giving thanks for the gifts and blessings that one has, like putting the needs of others before your own, like rejoicing in truth, like forgiving– not just erasing the tally sheet of wrongs endured, but tearing it up…forever. We are being transformed through the power of the Holy Spirit poured out in the undying love of Christ on the cross.

However, as Paul reminds us at the end of this passage, we are a "work in progress." This transformation, which began with our baptism into Christ, is ongoing. As we see clearly with the Corinthian congregation and in our own congregation, we do not always use our gifts and talents as God intended. We continue to be rebellious children, but when Jesus comes again, at the time of the completion, our transformation will be perfected. We will no longer see through a mirror dimly. We will be with God in Christ face-to-face. Until that time, God has gifted us through the power of the Holy Spirit, which is actively working within our lives.

What does this Spirit look like working here within the life of this congregation? It looks like the patience shown when the acolyte last Sunday took ten minutes to light the candles. It looks like allowing the members of the community in wheelchairs and on walkers and canes to be served first at the church luncheon three weeks ago. It looks like offering a ride to a member who can no longer see well, and doing this Sunday after Sunday. It looks like visiting those who are not able to attend church. It looks like youth taking the time to contribute special music for our Rally Day Sunday. It looks like a first-grader running outside, grabbing a wildflower, and breathlessly running to give it to his Sunday school teacher. It looks like listening to the view of other committee members, seeking the Lord's will through prayer and discernment over our own will. It looks like welcoming others into our church family even when they don't look the same as us. It looks like giving up the same seat we've sat in for the last ten years to welcome a visitor.

It looks like using our gifts and talents in loving service for the good of the body of Christ, even when, or especially when, it means self-giving, to further the mission of the church, to help a fellow church member, to help those in need to whom the church is ministering.

We do have many spiritual gifts: gifts of faith, sharing, comforting, consoling, singing, public reading, leadership, following, teaching, discerning, and many more. God's love has been poured out into our hearts through the Holy Spirit. It is through the power of the Holy Spirit that we are enabled to live our lives, as this church community, and as we walk outside this community. God in Christ through this love—surrounding us, filling us, transforming us—empowers and enables us to lead such lives. This is love in action. This is love in relationship.

1 Corinthians 13

Kirsi Stjerna

Jesus told his disciples to *bear fruit*. He called them to be the branches to bear fruit. As disciples, we also are called to be branches and bear fruit. But what is the fruit? What does it mean to bear fruit to God?

Christians have interpreted this to mean many things. Often the emphasis has been on the word *spiritual* to the extreme. People have tried to annihilate their humanity in order to become utterly spiritual. That has been the goal for centuries, as the church and spiritual teachers have proclaimed dualistic ideas, beliefs that our humanity, with all the "material" in the world, would be non-spiritual and thus less worthy and something to either "get rid off" or to discipline as much as possible in order to become a fruitful spirit and bear spiritual fruit.

This desire has led people to believe that good works and extreme spiritualism make one holy. Celibacy, isolation, fasting, self-torture, focusing on the "inside" and despising the "material" ordinary life are just a few of the practices people have thought might make them more spiritual. What happened in San Diego in 1997 with the suicide of thirty-nine cult members is an example of this kind of spirituality.

Another example of this kind of "divisive," extreme spirituality is a fifteenth-century woman, a saint: Catherine of Genoa was an aristocratic lady who wanted to free herself from everything "worldly," from bodily desires, and thus be free to fly to heaven as a pure spirit. To achieve this, she felt compelled to refrain from eating and to risk her life taking care of plague victims; she also saw it necessary to eat lice, lick smelly wounds of the sick, and withdraw from normal human contact...all this to kill her humanity and bear spiritual fruit to God. She has been revered as extremely spiritual, a saint.

Catherine, as odd as she may sound to us, was not alone, not a rarity at all in her time. Church history knows a number of women and men like her, who have become venerated as saints for their suffering, extraordinary spiritual zeal, and other spiritual "merits." Catherine of Siena is another famous spiritual person, another saint (also revered as the Doctor of the church for her passionate teachings), who humbled herself through great sacrifice to serve her Lord and fellow human beings. Before she literally starved to death, her great passion to bear fruit to God got her tangled up with the time's political controversies, even to reprimanding the pope himself!

As difficult as some aspects of these women's lives are for us to comprehend, there is something to be learned from their passion to be spiritual and alive spiritually. Also, we can relate to their ultimate concern: love. *We could say that these women were burning–and burnt–by their love.* Their actions were motivated by love, love of God–the way they understood and experienced it. Their spiritual power arose from their experience and practice of divine love, which they identified with their God, the source and object of all true love.

We could call these women "theologians of love." And we can be inspired by their passion to love, even if we cannot take it to heart to follow their exact paths. After all, we are not trying to become saints, but just learn to live and love as humans. We continue their struggle, however: how to be human and spiritual at the same time. Love seems to be the key.

How do we figure out in our lives *how* to be *spiritual* and bring fruit to God, and what has *love* got to do with it?

The first step in our spiritual journey could be to realize that there is more to life than the apparent, that without the spiritual dimension our lives aren't whole. That is a beginning of a spiritual journey, an eye-opener in a sense. Then we face the question of how the spiritual aspect manifests or is experienced in our everyday life. Where are the spiritual fruits in the midst of daily life?

Luther was one of the "common sense" theologians who expanded the notion of spirituality and spiritual fruitfulness. He had tried the extreme way and concluded that no works or rituals make us more spiritual–even if they may support our sense of spirituality. He broadened our perspectives on what is spiritual. He realized the blessedness of other-than-apparently spiritual aspects of our lives—such as doing the dishes, raising our children, doing our work, cultivating friendships, finding our place in life.

Marriage, to him, was a delightful new source of blessedness—and blessedness is already a spiritual fruit, whether we recognize it or not. Through his searching, Luther realized God is found in the midst of life—which makes everything we see, hear, touch, and breathe in spiritual and holy—therefore, it is simply in our human living that we bear fruit to God. God wants real fruit; life is real, concrete. We are spiritual *and* bear fruit when we see the spiritual connection in everything we are and do and have; we are spiritual when we are connected!

Spirituality comes from connectedness: with one's heart, with God and fellow-human beings, and with all the creation around us. Connectedness is the secret of being spiritual. And what is more "being connected" than loving?

Jesus' words about bearing fruit can be understood as a command to love. The idea of loving as a spiritual fruit and loving, connectedness, as a source of spirituality becomes clear from John's first letter: "Beloved let us love one another because love is from God; everyone who loves is born of God and knows God….if we love one another, God lives in us, and his love is perfected in us. By this we know that we abide in him and he in us, because he has given us of his Spirit…[*and this spirit*] God is love" (1 Jn. 4:7–16).

So, *love* connects us to God and other people, and to ourselves. Love *is* the greatest fruit, as Paul says to the Corinthians:

"Love is patient; love is kind; love is not envious or boastful or arrogant or rude. It does not insist on its own way; it is not irritable or resentful; it does not rejoice in wrongdoing, but rejoices in the truth. It bears all things, believes all things, hopes all things, endures all things. Love never ends. And now faith, hope, and love abide, these three; and the greatest of these is love." (1 Cor. 13:4–8).

As odd as it may seem, this famous passage was not originally part of a wedding sermon, but given as a piece of advice for all spiritual living and healthy discipleship in Christ. The implications of this advice are endless.

As described by Paul, love is much more than a sentiment, more than a specific good work. It is a way of living, and in it love is at the same time utterly concrete and most spiritual. Loving is like the thread of life, the electric cord permeating all our lives, making all we do and touch spiritual, giving us the touch of "saintliness," if you will, and thus pleasing to God.

Love leads us to do many mundane and oh-so-saintly things, anything from doing the laundry and changing the diapers to saying a prayer for our neighbor, swallowing an angry word, giving our attention to somebody in need, and making peace with our enemy. Love is creative; there is no end on this spiritual path; there are millions of ways to love, to produce the greatest of fruits.

If we look at the ways of relating to the world around us and of our decisions and actions as reflections of that fruit-producing love, we might gain a totally new perspective and attitude for our entire life. Namely, based on the Bible's wisdom, whatever we do out of love is spiritual, holy, pleasing to God, fruitful, and transforming. Loving acts and intentions are the most spiritual acts and the most concrete, real fruits of our lives.

There is nothing magical in being spiritual, living spiritually. We just heard a very clear guideline for spiritual, loving living in Paul's famous words on love. This beautiful elaboration of the golden rule to love in all possible creative ways illustrates the ample dimensions of holiness and loving living. It tells us who God is to us and sets a model for how we can also be loving spiritual beings, to one another, to God, and to ourselves.

Amen.

1 Corinthians 13

Kay Herzog Tostengard

A friend of mine in Seattle was sharing the trials and tribulations of his work life. He recently started working for a new manager and described this guy as a "dynamo." The manager would work through the night if need be to get his accounts in order, and he worked hard to make sure his clients were satisfied. His clients loved him. At first this manager was supportive of my friend, but as my friend's work started to show its strengths, the manager started to sabotage him. After months of negative comments and bitter criticism of his work by this manager, my friend went to the supervisor of both of them to try to find out what had gone wrong. The supervisor launched into a glowing assessment of this man's work, highlighting his achievements and gifts. My friend said he shrank into his chair thinking he was doomed to work in this hostile environment until he couldn't stand it anymore. He then asked, "Well, what's gone wrong? Why am I having trouble with this guy?" His supervisor knew right away: "He doesn't play well with others."

Remember that category on the report card? You can get an A in Language, a B+ in Math, do fine in Science and Art, but in grade school, the playground is where it all happens. Did you play well with others? All the qualities my friend's manager had are considered virtues in our day. He worked hard. He was smart and very funny. He'd go the extra mile, putting in his time for the sake of his clients. He was considered a decent man, the pillar-of-society type. He had a wife and children tucked away in the suburbs. My friend was disheartened to find that they shared the same faith—Christians, and Lutheran to boot. In all the ways that our society gives value to an individual, he would be considered virtuous. But he didn't play well with others.

This is what Paul in his writing to the Corinthians is taking to task. This long discourse on love in this thirteenth chapter has nothing to do with love as we construe it. While this piece of scripture seems to be the private domain of brides, it has more to do with Christian community and Christlike love than a sentimental wedding and a romantic marriage. When we read the whole of the book of Corinthians, we draw a very different picture of what is at stake for Paul as he writes. The congregation at Corinth was not unlike us in that they were very anxious to make distinctions between others and themselves. They were jockeying for position in their communities, trying to stand out as superior because they had particular gifts that made them special, more spiritual, more virtuous than the next person. But they couldn't play well with others. Paul even has to take them to task for their inexcusable behavior when they took communion, as we hear: "There are divisions among you...for when the time comes to eat, each of you goes ahead with your own supper, and one goes hungry and another becomes drunk" (1 Cor. 11:18–21). And yet, while all these factions existed, each individual thought of himself or herself as virtuous. Too often a person's virtue comes at the expense of Christian community. And Paul is riding down hard on them for that. "If you go in for heroics," he says, "looking for glitzy gifts that make you look good to others, always having the right words, prophesying the future, praying the most fervent prayers, even if you are willing to die the martyr's death, handing over your body so that you may boast, you are nothing. Because you are doing this all for yourself."

What this world would count as heroic or even virtuous acts are nothing if not given out of love. They don't fit into the Christian's vision or goal, the goal of building up the body of Christ. What appears to the world to be virtue, when used for yourself, when used for myself, is nothing. Virtue has a dark side; the evil of virtue is often a middle-class evil that can break down community if we think we possess virtue, more virtue than someone else. This is exactly the evil that led Christ to command us, to plead with us, to love our enemies. "You have heard that it was said, 'You shall love your neighbor and hate your enemy.' But I say to you, Love your enemy and pray for those who persecute you...For if you love those who love you, what reward do you have? Do not even the tax collectors do the same?" (Mt. 5:43–46). The one we consider the outsider, inferior to us because of our faith, our virtue, is one Christ has died to save, to redeem. Can you play with others, can you love others, even those very unlike you, and recognize in them the image of Christ that you, in God's graciousness, share with them?

The issue we're faced with is whether we'll settle for being just virtuous individuals, or will we be the body of Christ, in all its variety? If we want to find a band of like-minded individuals who share common qualities, such as political leanings, taste in worship, or educational backgrounds, then we will be virtuous individuals who have found one another. But if Paul's words are true, and I believe they are, and those virtues are nothing, that they in fact can destroy the body of Christ, then we want to be part of that body of Christ moved and shaped by the love that never ends.

Our virtues—along with Paul's list in the thirteenth chapter of Corinthians, prophesies, wise speech, and knowledge—will come to an end. Then all that will remain is Christ—who has fully known us, whose love for us has been patient and kind, not envious or boastful or arrogant or rude. This love has not insisted on its own way except to make sure that we would belong to him. In the extravagant love shown on the cross, Jesus has taken the insufferable weight of our very virtues, the virtues we would use to beat up and maim his own body, and his love bears all those things, and endures all those things. See, love never ends. Faith, hope, and love abide, but the greatest of these is love.

Amen.

The Love Stronger than Death: The Funeral of Sarah Elizabeth Desey

Dave von Schlichten

For a funeral especially, it is wisdom for us to imagine we are back at Golgotha on that first Good Friday. Imagine it. Maybe the air is heavy, chilly. Maybe the sky is swollen, ashen. Before us hangs Christ on the cross, the tree. His breathing comes in gasps with long pauses. He is gaunt, gray, transfigured, it seems, from triumphant king to tragic thing. This suffering seems godforsaken. Yet this is the love of God, this foolishness that is the true wisdom, the love stronger than death.

First Corinthians 13 teaches us that, without this love, the love of God in Christ Jesus, we have nothing, we are nothing. This love gives us eternal life, and this love shapes how we love one another. It is this love that enables us to rejoice today, even while we mourn Sarah's death.

The people of Corinth had trouble understanding the importance of this great love. They were competing with one another, ranking one another. There was a demonic division over who had the greater spiritual gift. In First Corinthians, Paul protests against this rivalry by saying that without this supreme love, speaking in tongues or having knowledge or any other gift amounts to nothing. For Paul, Christians are to be loving to one another, and loving one another means loving with the love of God in Christ as the foundation.

For us, too, all else is noise, nothing. How great our incomes are. Degrees we have obtained. What clothes we own. How thin we are. Even the good deeds we do. None of these is inherently bad, but without God's love, all is vanity.

Sarah knew this truth. Sarah loved according to God's love. She was tender and generous. For example, she loved to bake zucchini bread for shut-ins. Yesterday, during the viewing, her son told me that he considered her the wisest mother a person could have. I asked him why he'd said that. He replied, "Because she knew the value of bread." In general, God blessed us with a person who was often patient and kind with others, especially the sick. As a wife, mother, grandmother, great-grandmother, friend, and parishioner, she was not one we remember as having been envious, boastful, arrogant, or rude. She was rarely irritable or resentful. She did not rejoice in wrongdoing, but rejoiced in the truth. She labored to live God's love before all people and all events, all things.

May we always remember her goodness, for through her we experienced love as described in 1 Corinthians 13, the love based in God's love. Indeed, may we remember that her love came from God's love, which has come first and which meets us at the end and which sustains us in the meantime. It is God's love as expressed in Christ on the tree that frees us from sin and death so we can live as children who love according to God's love. It is God's love that is our foundation, supporting us and shaping our actions, words, and thoughts so that we seek to build each other up, not puff up. This is the love stronger than death, this love of God that empowers our love, just as it empowered Sarah's love.

During these days of grief, we need this love in a way that helps us heal. When we see the emptiness, feel the emptiness of the house, the pew, we may feel the ache of grief. We are called to edify one another with loving acts rooted in the love of God in Christ on the tree. We can listen patiently to one another's memories. We can hold each other. We can bake casseroles and pies for one another. We can call one another and send cards. We are to pray for one another. Turn to 1 Corinthians 13. See to what love God calls us.

In his short story "A Small, Good Thing," Raymond Carver tells us of two parents whose young son is hit by a car and killed. Their grief is deep and forceful, like a swollen river. Who can console them? Then, at the story's end, the parents have an unusual encounter with a baker. The baker is not good with words. He does not speak any sympathy or comfort. Instead, he sits the parents down and shares with them sweet rolls and bread. The rolls and the bread—the fragrance, the sweetness, the chewiness, the buoyancy—these small, good things comfort the bereaved parents. May we do likewise.

As we love one another, above all else we are to remind and assure one another that the love of God in Christ gives us unending life. Because of the love of God in Christ, we have hope. Because of the love of God in Christ, we have faith in God's faithfulness to us. Because of the love of God in Christ, we have the unassailable assurance that eternal life is for Sarah and all of us who have accepted the free gift of salvation. We are to remind one another of this love stronger than death, the love that gives us eternal life.

"Love never ends," Paul writes. Thanks be to God! All else—the cars, the house, the computer, the knowledge, the talents—someday will be abolished. But the love of God in Christ cannot be abolished, because God will not allow it even to be shaken. We have the immovable guarantee that eventually Sarah and all of Christ's siblings will see God with overpowering, luminous clarity. First Corinthians 13 promises that we will see face-to-face. Imagine seeing God face-to-face. The eyes of God, sleepless, unblinking, welling up with moist compassion and joy for us, will be upon us always, so close we will see our reflections in them. God will abide with us and we with God, death destroyed, forgotten.

In the musical *Les Miserables,* the characters, no matter how virtuous, suffer. The hero especially, Jean Val Jean, spends his life fleeing from those who want to throw him unjustly into prison. There is much chaos and sorrow. A happy ending seems impossible. Yet, as Jean Val Jean lies dying, he is summoned to eternal happiness in heaven. Now the stage fills with characters, including the many who have died, and now they sing together as one that they "will live again in freedom in the garden of the Lord." It is the love stronger than death that composes their song. Sarah's life was far happier, but the final song is the same: She lives again in freedom in the garden of the Lord.

Today, grieve. To do so is part of loving Sarah and giving thanks to God for her goodness. In that grief, though, let us build up one another according to the love that God has given us through Christ's sacrifice. And all the while, in all that we do, let us always remember, let us never forget, that even after we exhale our final breath, we shall live, God's love forever stronger than death.

Amen.

The Marriage of Debra Torrone and Robert Kilkenny

Raewynne J. Whiteley

You have to look hard if you want to find an anywhere-near-good definition of love. The dictionary will tell you that it's a noun that has been around in its current form since the twelfth century and that it has to do with affection, desire, and admiration. Hallmark would have us believe that it's all about plump red hearts and the flutter of romance. But it's not always quite so appealing.

If you listen to Elton John, you'll discover that love is a cannibal; folk singer Connie Kaldor says love is a truck; for William Shakespeare, it's a fever. And according to the http://www.Mommiesontheweb.com Web site, love is scaring away monsters in the middle of the night.

Love is a mixed-up, tangled kind of thing, and sometimes it's difficult to get a hold on what it's all about—even on a day like today, when we are, to all intents and purposes, gathering together to celebrate love...whatever that is.

And perhaps part of our problem is that we tend to look at love in the abstract. We imagine it as some philosophical concept that magically joins with our emotions to produce this warm, happy feeling deep inside. We talk about falling in love as if there is some idyllic state that could protect us from the all-too-often-ugly realities of our ordinary lives. And that may be true for fairy tale weddings, but none of us live fairy tale lives. Life is as complex and muddled a mixture as love is—which is why it matters so much to find a somewhere-near-good definition of love.

And I think where we might find it is not in dictionaries or love songs or poetry or even on the Web. Where we can find it is in the ordinary, everyday lives of the people like us, people who have taken the chance, made a decision to pour their hearts and minds and souls, every fiber of their being, into one another.

Because love, it seems to me, is a whole lot more about what we do than what we feel; it's what we think and decide, what we choose and what we reject. It's the small things as much as the big ones, the ordinary as well as the exciting. Love is about different sleeping patterns and standards of cleanliness, about who empties the trash and who cleans the bathroom. It's about mood swings and shopping, grief and celebration.

Love is waiting at home with an overcooked meal, or hearing the phone ring and ring in an empty house. It's when you look at your partner and realize that she is not perfect, and neither are you. It's about discovering that you are both different, and learning to love those differences. It's about discovering unexpected maturity and unexpected childishness, about growing together even when nothing seems to change.

Love is learning to care for each other's families, learning to laugh when they bug you, learning to cry when they hurt. And it's learning to carve out a new space for yourselves as a couple, and later, as a family. It's about having new friends whom you would never have imagined or welcomed, and about friends who are not shared, but belong to the two separate worlds that this love has so strangely brought together. It's managing that tricky balance between couplehood and individuality, interdependence and independence, togetherness and freedom.

Love is about learning to face disagreement openly, not smothering conflict, but listening, waiting, working together so that out of the pain can come new understanding and new life. It's about knowing the difference between the passions and dreams that make you who you are and the things that you would like but that are a whole lot less important than your life together.

Love is about holding your partner close when he is finding things tough, even if you don't quite understand what the problem is. About not always demanding an explanation but trusting one another, not being afraid of honesty, and being honest about your fears.

Love is doing the grocery shopping and eating McDonald's when you thought you were going to have a romantic dinner, until work intervened. It's about not getting overly obsessed about whether you should squeeze the toothpaste from the middle or the bottom of the tube, about not getting hung up when you arrive places awkwardly early or embarrassingly late. It's about taking the bad along with the good, about believing in new beginnings, accepting apologies, and offering forgiveness.

Love is about choosing to build a relationship that is more like a rubber band than a porcelain figurine. Porcelain is beautiful, but fragile. Your love needs to be practical and elastic, able to stretch and to wrap itself around your lives.

All that can sound kind of overwhelming. And yet what it is all about is taking small steps, the tiny decisions, day by day, that add up to a life of love. The wedding vows you make this evening are central, but tonight is also just one decision among many. Because love is about choosing to choose each other, again, and again, and again.

Sometimes that choice will not be easy. Other times it will be the occasion for wonder and delight. Most times it will take courage and commitment.

Which is why we spend the last part of this service praying for you. Not because we think these prayers are some sort of magical spell that will keep your love safe, but because we trust that the love of God will shape and fill your love for the rest of your lives. For it's that love that shapes our love, and it's that love that is described in these words:

> Love is patient; love is kind; love is not envious or boastful or arrogant or rude. It does not insist on its own way; it is not irritable or resentful; it does not rejoice

in wrongdoing, but rejoices in the truth. It bears all things, believes all things, hopes all things, endures all things. Love never ends.

I'm not sure we can find a better definition than that.

Epiphany 4, 1998

Joseph Wolf

Grace to you and peace from God our Father and the Lord Jesus Christ. Amen.

We are soon to be awash in "love." Florists are hurrying to get ready for their busiest day of the year. Schoolkids are scooping up boxes of cards to exchange in classrooms across America. Candy makers are on a "sugar high" as they anticipate all the boxes of chocolates that will be given out in a couple of weeks.

February is the month of "love"—the hearts of the young will go aflutter when the sweet words are whispered in their ears, "Will you be my valentine?"

And hearts will be broken when no such words are heard. Cupid, the story goes, will be out and about taking aim with his arrows, spreading a dose of "love" across the land. Now hold on. Before you go thinking that this preacher's planning to deride, belittle, and otherwise make fun of Valentine's Day, just as he does Christmas, I'll have you know something: I like Valentine's Day. I've even been known to get my wife a little something on February 14. I think it's great that for one day, at least, we can be intentional about showing our love for others, even if in rather cursory and sentimental ways.

So what's the problem? Well, the problem's not so much Valentine's Day, but it's that little four-letter word, *l-o-v-e, love*. Our culture has so twisted and perverted that little word that we may not know exactly what it is we're saying when we say "love." "All you need is love," sang the Beatles in the 1960s. Well, just what does that mean? Should we all be holding hands and engaging in group hugs? Part of the problem, it seems, is with the English language. In English there is but one word for love, and this word *l-o-v-e* must make do for a multiplicity of meanings: sexual desire, the love between family members and friends, and the kind of love that Saint Paul writes about in his First Letter to the Corinthians, the love of Christ that we can share for one another.

In Greek, you see, which is the language of the New Testament, there are three words that can mean love in its varying meanings. To help you grasp this, we'll use some visual aids this morning. The first Greek word for love is *eros*. Now many of you are familiar with this word, because from this Greek word comes the English word *erotic*. *Eros* denotes the kind of love that has to do with sexual desire and attraction. This is the romantic "falling in love" love. It is "love at first sight" love. It is the kind of love that causes sweaty palms and sleepless nights. *Eros* is Valentine's Day love, Cupid and all.

But any of you who have been "in love" in this romantic way know how notoriously short-lived are our feelings of romantic love. It comes on us quickly and like a high fever burns briskly. But over time, and with some Tylenol, the temperature returns to normal. In fact, researchers suggest that at least part of what we call "falling in love" can be attributed to the presence in the body of a chemical called "phenylethylamine." It is a form of natural amphetamine. The problem is, the researchers have found that we build up a tolerance to this chemical in about two to four years. *Eros,* "falling in love" love, can be a wonderful thing, but it is a fleeting thing as well.

The next Greek word for love is *phileo*. If you look closely, you may recognize this word as well. It forms the first part of the name of our state's largest city, Philadelphia, which is the city of "brotherly love."

Phileo means to treat someone as "one of one's own people." It is familial love, the love between spouses, parents and children, between siblings, even between friends and neighbors. *Phileo* is the love of those bound tightly together by family and community ties. *Phileo* is enjoyable love, companionship, collegiality. Most of us have experienced *phileo* love, either through our families or through friends in the community. The trouble with *phileo,* as we humans express it at least, is that it many times lasts only as long as relationships are problem free. You've seen it happen before. A person gets into trouble, or does something stupid, and his or her friends leave in droves. But there is, writes Saint Paul, "a still more excellent way."

> If I speak in the tongues of mortals and of angels, but do not have love, I am a noisy gong or a clanging cymbal. And if I have prophetic powers, and understand all mysteries and all knowledge, and if I have all faith, so as to remove mountains, but do not have love, I am nothing.

The word Paul uses here for love is not *eros*, nor is it *phileo*. Paul now uses the Greek word *agape* for love. Before I go any further, I want to stress that *eros* and *phileo* are legitimate "kinds of love." How boring life would be without the adventure and excitement of romantic love. How empty and shallow would life be with out *phileo*, without the love between spouses and parents and children and our friends and neighbors. But without *agape* love, life would not only be boring and barren, it would be well nigh impossible.

Agape is the love that made you and me. It is the love of the Creator for the creation, the love of our Maker who made us. It is the creative love of God that surrounded us before we were even formed in our mother's womb; it is this love that remains with you now to deliver you. Unlike *eros*, which desires another for self-satisfaction, *agape*, the love of God for us, seeks nothing for us but a life of freedom. Unlike *phileo*, which can evaporate at the first sign of trouble, *agape*, the love of God for us, never ends.

No one has described it better than Paul:

> Love is patient; love is kind, love is not envious or boastful or arrogant or rude. It does not insist on its own way; it is not irritable or resentful; it does not rejoice in wrongdoing, but rejoices in the truth. It bears all things, believes all things, hopes all things, endures all things.

This is the love of God for us, the love that made us, and also the love that redeems us. *Agape* is the love of Christ for you; it is love in the shape of a cross, a seeking, striving love that searches until it finds you, no matter what life has brought you thus far, no matter what mistakes you have made, no matter how many friends have left you. It is a love that will not let you go.

If you have ever been loved in this way, you'll never forget it, or you shouldn't. I like the story about a couple celebrating their fortieth wedding anniversary with a quiet dinner for two. The wife raises up her champagne glass to toast and says, "In spite of everything!" Saint Valentine might not approve. Saint Paul would understand. In spite of everything, God has loved you and has brought you to this point in your life. In spite of everything, here you are on this Sunday morning hearing the good news again.

In spite of everything—that's *agape* love, the love of Christ that outlasts everything—all our great ideas, all our boneheaded stunts, all our failed relationships, all our bodies growing old, love that outlasts everything—even death.

Pray that you too can love in this way. Pray that God would grant you grace to take the risk to love in this way, this most excellent way in which God has first loved you.

Amen.

NOTES

Chapter 2: Preaching 1 Corinthians 13

[1] *The Rubáiyát of Omar Khayyám,* trans. Edward FitzGerald, 1859.

[2] For an in-depth look at the preparation and preaching of the wedding sermon see Susan K. Hedahl, *Preaching the Wedding Sermon* (St. Louis: Chalice Press, 1999).

[3] Thomas G. Long, "The Focus and Function of the Sermon," in *The Witness of Preaching* (Louisville, Ky.: Westminster/John Knox Press, 1989), 86.

[4] Ibid.

[5] John Henry Newman, *Practical and Parochial Sermons,* vols. 1–8 (London: Scribner, Welford, & Co., New York, 1968).

Chapter 3: Voices from the Historical Pulpit

[1] John Calvin, *Commentary on the Epistles of Paul the Apostle to the Corinthians,* trans. John Pringle (Grand Rapids, Mich.: Wm. B. Eerdmans, 1948; original, Edinburgh: Calvin Translation Society, 1848), 3.

[2] Sermon 162A from *The Works of Saint Augustine: A Translation for the 21st Century, Sermons III/5 (148183 on the New Testament,* trans. and notes by Edmund Hill, ed. John E. Rotelle (New Rochelle, N. Y.: New City Press, 1992), 152–66.

[3] Ibid., 154, 155.

[4] John Chrysostom, "Homily XXXIII" in *A Select Library of the Nicene and Post-Nicene Fathers,* ed. Phil Schaff, vol. 12 (New York: The Christian Literature Company, 1889), 194–201.

[5] Ibid., 194.

[6] John Chrysostom, "Homily XXXIV" in *A Select Library of the Nicene and Post-Nicene Fathers,* ed. Phil Schaff, vol. 12 (New York: The Christian Literature Company, 1889), 201–8.

[7] Ibid., 202.

[8] Ibid., 204.

[9] Saint Caesarius of Arles, Sermon 23, "An Exhortation to Observe or Preserve Charity, That No One Can Really Excuse Himself for not Possessing True Charity. The Addition of a Few Ideas of St. Augustine From a Sermon On Charity," in *Saint Caesarius of Arles Sermons,* vol. 1 of *The Fathers of the Church,* trans. Sister Mary Magdaleine Mueller, O.S.F (New York: Fathers of the Church, Inc., 1956), 118–23.

[10] Ibid., 118.

[11] Ibid., 122–23.

[12] Saint Caesarius, "Sermon #29," in *Saint Caesarius of Arles Sermons,* vol. 1, *The Fathers of the Church,* trans. Sister Mary Magdaleine Mueller, O.S.F (New York: Fathers of the Church, Inc., 1956), 144.

[13] Ibid., 145.

[14] Ibid., 147.

[15] Baldwin of Ford, "Tractate XIV, On the Order of Charity," in *Baldwin of Ford, Spiritual Tractates,* vol. 2, trans. David N. Bell (Kalamazoo, Mich.: Cistercian, 1986), 141ff.
[16] Ibid., 142.
[17] Ibid., 146.
[18] Ibid., 151.
[19] *St. Bernard's Sermons,* vol. 3, trans. a Priest of Mount Melleray (Westminster, Md.: The Carroll Press, 1950), 39–50.
[20] Ibid., 41.
[21] Ibid., 42.
[22] Ibid., 46.
[23] Ibid., 50.
[24] Ibid., 50.
[25] John Wycliffe, "Charity," in *20 Centuries of Great Preaching,* vol. 1 (Waco, Tex.: Word Books, 1971), 242.
[26] Ibid., 244.
[27] Thomas Aquinas in *The Preacher's Encyclopedia, From Advent to Quinquagesima,* comp. and ed. Angel Cardinal Herrera; English version trans. and ed. Msgr. David Greenstock (Westminster, Md.: The Newman Press, 1965), 699–700.
[28] Information from the Paul Fields, Meeter Center, Calvin College, Grand Rapids, Michigan, December, 2000.
[29] John Calvin, *Commentary on The Epistles of Paul the Apostle to The Corinthians,* vol. 1, trans. and ed. John Pringle (London: 1848; repr. Grand Rapids: Wm. B. Eerdmans, 1948), 426–27.
[30] Count Nikolaus Ludwig von Zinzendorf, "Lecture V, that Aspect of Faith which Actually Makes One so Blessedly Happy," in *Nine Public Lectures on Important Subjects in Religion,* trans. and ed. by George W. Forell (Iowa City: University of Iowa Press, 1973), 56.
[31] Ibid., 48–49.
[32] Ibid., 51.
[33] Ibid., 56.
[34] Ibid., 57.
[35] Jonathan Edwards, "Christian Love As Manifested In The Heart And Life," in *20 Centuries of Great Preaching,* vol. 3, ed. Clyde Fant, Jr., and William M. Pinson, Jr. (Waco, Tex.: Word Books, 1971), 82–102.
[36] Ibid., 89.
[37] Ibid., 90.
[38] Ibid.
[39] Ibid.
[40] Ibid., 91.
[41] Ibid.
[42] Ibid., 102.
[43] John M. Wesley, "On Charity," Sermon 97, vol. 2 of *Sermons on Several Occasions* (New York: Lane & Tippett, 1847), 280.
[44] Ibid., 280.
[45] Ibid., 283.
[46] Ibid., 285–86.
[47] George Whitefield, "The Great Duty of Charity Recommended," in *Works of the Reverend George Whitefield* (London: 1771–1772). Quote found on

Internet resource, at http://reformed.org/documents/Whitefield/WITF_047.html in August 2001.

[48]Ibid., 7.
[49]Ibid., 3.
[50]Ibid., 4.
[51]Ibid., 9.
[52]Rev. H. P. Liddon, "The First Five Minutes After Death," No. 1,098 in *The Penny Pulpit, New Series* (London: F. Davis, n.d.), 25–32.
[53]Ibid., 27–28.
[54]Ibid., 30–31.
[55]Ibid., 31–32.
[56]Anonymous, "The Kindly Offices of the Three Cardinal Christian Virtues at the Burial of Christians," in *"I Am the Resurrection and the Life": A Book of Funeral Sermons by Lutheran Pastors,* 6th ed. (St. Louis: Concordia, 1916), 238–39.
[57]Ibid., 241.
[58]Ibid., 243.
[59]Ibid., 245.
[60]Phillips Brooks, "The Knowledge of God," in *Twenty Sermons,* 4th series (New York: E. P. Dutton & Company, 1887), 280–96.
[61]Ibid., 296.
[62]Ibid., 295–96.
[63]Henry Drummond, "The Greatest Thing in the World," in *Treasury of the World's Great Sermons,* comp. Warren W. Wiersbe (Grand Rapids: Kregel, 1977), 178–86.
[64]Ibid., 179.
[65]Ibid., 179–80.
[66]Ibid., 179.
[67]Ibid., 183.
[68]Ibid., 186.
[69]John Henry Newman, "The Centrality of Charity," in *The Preaching of John Henry Newman,* ed. W. D. White (Philadelphia: Fortress Press, 1969), 95–105.
[70]Ibid., 98.
[71]Ibid., 100.
[72]Ibid., 101.
[73]Ibid.
[74]Ibid., 104.
[75]Henry Ward Beecher, "Sovereignty and Permanence of Love," in *The Original Plymouth Pulpit,* vol. 7 (Boston: The Pilgrim Press, 1872), 121.
[76]G. H. Morrison, "Mystery," in *Sunrise: Addresses from a City Pulpit* (London: Hodder and Stoughton, 1904), 12–20.
[77]Ibid., 17, 19–20.
[78]Harry Emerson Fosdick, "The Most Durable Power in the World," in *Successful Christian Living: Sermons on Christianity Today* (New York: Harper & Brothers, 1937), 86–96.
[79]Ibid., 88.
[80]Ibid., 90.
[81]Ibid., 92.
[82]Ibid., 94.

[83] Ibid., 95.
[84] Ibid., 96.
[85] George Hodges, "The Quality of Charity," in George Hodges, *Year of Grace* (New York: Thomas Whittaker, 1906), 132.
[86] Ibid., 134.
[87] Ibid., 137.
[88] Ibid., 142–43.
[89] J. H. Jowett, "The Modesty of Love," in *Brooks by The Traveller's Way: Twenty-Six Weeknight Addresses* (New York: Hodder and Stoughton, n.d.), 201–9).
[90] Ibid., 204.
[91] Ibid., 206–7.
[92] Ibid., 208–9.
[93] George Buttrick, "Knowledge and Love," in *Sermons Preached in a University Church* (New York: Abingdon Press, 1959), 139–46.
[94] Ibid., 142.
[95] Ibid.
[96] Ibid., 143.
[97] Ibid.
[98] Ibid., 144.
[99] Ibid.
[100] Ibid., 146.
[101] Karl Barth, "Aids for the Preacher," in *Church Dogmatics,* index vol., ed. G. W. Bromiley and T. F. Torrance (Edinburgh: T. & T. Clark Ltd., 1977), 345–46.
[102] William Edwin Sangster, "When Hope is Dead–Hope On!" in *20 Centuries of Great Preaching,* vol. 11, ed. Clyde E. Fant, Jr., and William M. Pinson, Jr. (Waco, Texas: Word Books, 1971), 363–69.
[103] Ibid., 366.
[104] Karl Rahner, "A Thing That is Transparent Must Be Empty," in *The Great Church Year: The Best of Karl Rahner's Homilies, Sermons, and Meditations,* ed. Albert Raffelt (New York: Crossroads, 1995), 244–46.
[105] Ibid., 245.
[106] Ibid.
[107] Walter J. Burghardt, S.J., "You Have Ravished My Heart," in *To Christ I Look: Homilies At Twilight* (New York: Paulist Press, 1989), 180–85.
[108] Ibid., 183.
[109] Robert Edward Luccock, "When Love Has the Last Word," in *If God Be For Us; Sermons on the Gift of the Gospel* (New York: Harper & Brothers, 1954), 71.
[110] Paul Tillich, *The Shaking of the Foundations* (New York: Charles Scribner's Sons, 1948), 108–13.
[111] Ibid., 112–13.
[112] Fleming Rutledge, "The Love Olympics Go to Jerusalem," in *The Bible and the New York Times* (Grand Rapids: Wm. Eerdmans, 1998), 80–85.
[113] Ibid., 85.
[114] Martin Luther King, Jr., "Paul's Letter to American Christians," in *The Strength to Love* (New York: Harper & Row Publishers, 1963), 127.
[115] Ibid., 133–34.

Chapter 4: Contemporary Sermons on 1 Corinthians 13

[1] For this paragraph, I am indebted to Richard Hays, *First Corinthians,* Interpretation: A Bible Commentary for Preaching and Teaching (Louisville: John Knox Press, 1997), 226–28.

[2] Emil Brunner, "The Temporal and the Eternal," in *The Great Invitation and Other Sermons by Emil Brunner,* trans. Harold Knight (Philadelphia: Westminster Press, 1955), 17–25.

[3] Paraphrase and quote from Margery Williams Bianco, *The Velveteen Rabbit: Or, How Toys Become Real* (New York: Avon Books, 1975).

[4] Martin Luther, "Sunday Before Lent," in Martin Luther, *Epistle Sermons* (Minneapolis: Luther Press, 1908), 119–32. Scripture references are taken from this edition.